Losing my Best Friend

Thoughtful support for those affected by dog bereavement or pet loss

D0167073

Jeannie Wycherley

Jeanniewycherley.co.uk
Copyright © 2018 Jeannie Wycherley
Bark at the Moon Books
All rights reserved
No part of this book may be reproduced or transmitted in any
form or by any means without written permission from the
copyright holder.
ISBN-10: 0995781826
ISBN-13: 978-0995781825

This book is written in English (UK), and therefore British
spelling has been used throughout.

DEDICATION

This book is dedicated with eternal love
to the memories of
Barney
Buttons
Diggs
Dirk
Pickles
Poppy
Sara

and Herbie

And to any best friends you, the reader, have loved and
lost.

*Cherish your memories, no matter how painful,
and your friend will live on in your heart for
always ...*

CONTENTS

Losing My Best Friend

Author's note

When I first published *Losing my Best Friend*, I did so to mark the first anniversary since Herbie had passed. I really did not expect the book to sell as well, or as consistently as it has done. I would have been ecstatic if just one person had found it useful, but in fact, many readers have been in touch one way or another to thank me and let me know I helped to validate their pain.

I am gratified that so many of my readers have come from across the pond, in the USA, even though this book originates in the UK. At the end of the day, we all love our pets the same way, don't we?

I have been asked numerous times to create a hard copy, so here it is, by popular demand! I have also included blank pages here and there, so that you can write your own thoughts and memories down.

I have largely left the text of the original untouched, because I think it helps the reader if it is written from a more immediate point of view.

I would like to rededicate this version to include Satin, my Staffy x Whippet. At fourteen and a half, she has a little joint stiffness, she's a bit hard of hearing and she has a bit of a cough. Herbie's best friend may well be joining him at the Bridge soon enough. Reunited, friends forever.

To all our beloved hounds, run free, run happy, until we meet again.

Jeannie Wycherley, 20th April 2018

FOREWORD

I lost my best friend on 29th July 2016.

As I write this I am coming up to all his final anniversaries.

My Facebook memories tell me daily about our fun times over the years, however, over the past few months or so, they have also started to remind me of my increasing concern for him twelve months ago. There. I've written two sentences and even though he has been gone for a substantial amount of time I have a knot in my throat and tears in my eyes.

If that resonates with you, then please understand that YOU are exactly the reason I am going to plough through this heartache and finish this book.

I have asked other dog owners, whom I am connected to, to tell me their stories too. Together we'll share what it is like to lose your best friend and we'll discuss ways we have found to help us cope. The intention is that this little book will gently help and support you, and then you and I and all bereaved dog owners everywhere will move forwards together.

Please bear in mind I'm not claiming this book will do any of the following:

- Take away your pain
- Bring you closure
- Mend your broken heart.

The thing is, I'm not a grief counsellor, a therapist, a

behaviourist or anything else. I trained as a historian, then I taught for 16 years, and now I run a gift shop with my husband and I write part time. My expertise stems only from the fact that I'm a dog owner, and I fell totally in love with a very special boy. I've had twelve months to experience dog bereavement and consider the attitudes (of myself and others) towards my own grief.

What this book sets out to do is:

- Show you that you're not alone on this journey
- Prove you're not abnormal
- It will make you cry
- It will tell you it's okay to cry
- It will offer some ideas for you to think about that may help you through your grief
- It will point out other places that offer help for pet bereavement

HOW TO USE THIS BOOK

I've divided the book into short sections. Some of them are anecdotal, some are practical, and some of them are suggestive or reflective. You can skip any parts you like. It may be that this book won't help you at all, and I'm really sorry. Please know that I understand that some grief cannot be eased.

Are you ready?

Let me start by telling you about Herbie.

1. HERBIE LONGFELLOW ALDERDICE

'Sooty', as he was known at the time, was born on 9th September 2006, and was one of seven puppies. Dad was a Bedlington Terrier, and Mum was a Collie x Lurcher, making Sooty a Bedlington x Collie Lurcher. He grew a little larger than a whippet, but never as tall as a greyhound. He was slight, but furry with lovely curls. He didn't moult so he had to have furcuts. Both his groomers, Yvonne in Chaddesden, Derby and Ali in Talaton, East Devon loved him.

But I can tell you now, and I know you'll understand, nobody loved him as much as me.

I had rescued an elderly Bedlington Whippet, named Toby, in 2004, whom I had doted on for his final few years. He was nine when I found him at a local kennel, and I think I gave him a good few years of life. It really hurt to let him go when he was put to sleep in October 2006 after a short illness. I found myself feeling lonely and desperately sad. I asked my vet at the time if this feeling of grief was normal, after all – he was 'just a dog' - and she said to me, "It's all the love you still have that you want to give him. It has nowhere to go."

In spite of my husband's assertion that it was too soon, I started looking around for another companion. Looking back, I can see that I was searching for Toby. I went to the kennels I had rescued him from, but he wasn't there. I tried the local papers. Nothing. Then I found an online selling site for dogs and puppies.

Now I'm not suggesting that the buying and selling of puppies online is a good thing or a bad thing. It is under regulated and open to abuse – I know that. But I was lucky. Less than ten days after I'd lost Toby, my husband and I ventured into deepest rural Lincolnshire and found Darren and his puppies tucked well off the beaten track on a smallholding. Mum was gorgeous and of course the puppies were so cute. Aren't they always? The house smelled of incense and wood smoke and was clean and tidy, and Darren was a lovely guy who worked on the land with his dog.

I had the pick of the litter because I was first to view and I couldn't decide between the dark grey and the black one. I knew the dark grey would become lighter and I was worried that I was still looking for Toby who had been 'blue'. I must have changed my mind a dozen times, to the amusement of my husband, Darren and his girlfriend. But we were happy enough, playing with the puppies and drinking tea.

After much umming and ahhing, I decided there was something about the dark grey chap that really called to me. Yes, young Sooty, was appealing. He liked to go off and explore on his own, but he kept coming back to me. Eventually I did choose Sooty and we left him to grow up with his Mum for another few weeks.

Two weeks later, I was in a supermarket doing the big weekly shop, when Darren phoned to tell me that Sooty was ready to leave Mum. I wanted to abandon my trolley and head back to Lincolnshire then and there, after all it was only a four-hour round trip, but my long-suffering husband put his foot down and we waited another few days. Actually, that's a lie. I think we waited twenty-four hours. That's all I could manage.

It was the end of October and the country was bathed in beautiful and unseasonably warm sunshine. The puppies were playing in the garden in a makeshift enclosure. Mum raced to meet us and little, adventurous Sooty climbed over the foot-high fence to bound joyously around.

Be still my beating heart. My love affair with him had begun.

All through the journey home I cosied up with Sooty in the back of the car and talked to him. He was quite calm and didn't cry at all. John and I bandied some names about, because we didn't really like Sooty. I went through all the letters of the alphabet and when I reached H and Herbie, we knew that was the one. It suited him, not least because he smelt of incense.

From the moment I collected him, to – well to now as you read this – he has occupied my very being. I don't know whether I will ever stop feeling him inside my soul. He occupies space within me, constantly.

Back then I was working full time, as was my husband, but we had teenagers in and out of the house and there was usually someone at home. Herbie and I went to puppy classes and spent good quality time together in the evenings and at weekends. I would leave early in the morning, do my 8 hours and dash home – always intent on getting back to him. I didn't want to go out anywhere without him. I just wanted to be with him. He lit up my life in every way.

We spent our summer holidays camping and walking the dogs, sharing time with them. There were occasions when John and I travelled abroad and initially we used kennels, but the first couple of incarcerations were so stressful (for both Herbie and for me) that I needed an alternative. I asked around at work, feeling tentative about foisting my dog on anyone, but to my surprise a work colleague offered to dog sit him, and from that moment on he had a pair of new fans. He was equally as devoted to his Auntie Debbie and his Uncle Rob as he was to me.

He was as good as gold, was Herbie. He was intelligent (collie), placid (greyhound), but extremely vocal (Bedlington). He loved to run, and boy could he run. He ran in great sweeping circles whenever he had the chance. His other hobbies were sniffing, sleeping and licking his 'bits'. I never had him neutered, I always wanted pups. Grandpups. Herbie was very fond of his manliness, and he liked to keep everything sparkly clean.

He was a stickler for time-keeping too. He knew exactly what should happen and when. He knew the time of morning walkies (no lie-ins for us on a weekend), he knew what he should have for breakfast and when he could expect treats. In the evening he would get up from wherever he was lying (usually on the sofa, upside down) and head for the back door. Wee wees and bedtime. He loved his routines.

He trusted me with everything. I could do whatever I liked or needed to. He would nibble horrible drugs out of my hand, allow me to clean wounds, I could de-tick him, I could wash his face and eyes, take thorns out of his paws. He remained calm and loving always.

It's fair to say I was obsessed with him. I talked to him all the time, and he listened. He watched my face. We could communicate merely by me smiling, nodding my head or cocking an eyebrow. We were so empathetic of each other. If I was annoyed, he would hide – not that I EVER took my angst out on him. If I was sad, he wanted to snuggle with me, or kiss my face. When I was happy he was joyful. Similarly, I could anticipate what he needed or what he was feeling, just by watching him or touching him.

He was my everything.

In the Spring of 2012 I was suffering with stress, extreme anxiety, and chronic depression. I needed to take some time out from work and when my GP signed me off, it allowed me to be at home with Herbie for a few weeks. It was very healing just to chill together. I had always wanted to write and now I had the time, so I did just that. He would settle under my desk. It was wonderful to be constant companions.

I had to go back to work though, and I missed him so much. When my employment situation didn't look like improving, my manager offered me redundancy. In the heat of that moment I felt so many things, humiliation, disappointment and fear – but the clarity of the thought 'to be at home with Herbie' shone out like a beacon. I knew it was what I wanted and needed.

And it was. Initially I looked for other work, but what I really desired was to work from home, and within a few months I was earning enough from copywriting just to get by. I found some great clients and kept at it.

Unfortunately, I couldn't earn enough for my husband and I to keep our mortgage going so we opted for a big life change. We seized the opportunity with both hands, sold our house, downsized and moved to Devon in the south west of the UK (home in my case, where my family are).

Finding rented accommodation with three dogs is difficult, and we scrutinized properties for proximity to walks. The dogs were always our priority. I was worried they wouldn't settle, but actually they did, very quickly. I think Herbie missed his sofa more than anything. We used to joke about that. The cottage we moved into was tiny, so we brought very little furniture with us. I did bring the end cushion from the sofa with me though, and he liked to lie with his head on that.

I still have that cushion, here in my study.

Eighteen months later, circumstances forced another move on us, this time up into the forest, or the Land of Clouds and Forest as I thought of it. Perfect for dogs, so much space to run around. I continued with my writing, and by now Herbie had a bed set up permanently beneath my desk. When I reached a point where I needed to think, I would pause, and automatically put my left hand out. Herbie would nestle into me. My left hand and his head, a permanent bond.

Ah, and now I have to pause and swallow.

Herbie had an issue with his teeth. I am a bit of an over-bearing Mum where dog teeth are concerned, because

Toby, my Bedlington Whippet had terrible teeth that should have been taken out long before I rescued him, and his eventual death from kidney failure may have been as a direct result of an issue with bad teeth. Naturally I checked with my vet about Herbie's teeth and she agreed he could do with a clean. As he wasn't due any other procedures, we put it off, but eventually in 2015 I found a tooth in his basket, showed it to my vet, and she agreed he needed a dental clean as soon as possible.

Of course I was worried, but I figured this was routine. He would have the little operation and be a bit sore, and I would keep his teeth properly clean and everything would continue. Herbie was going to live forever after all.

The procedure under general anaesthetic resulted in three more teeth being removed. He didn't need to stay overnight. He came home and I looked after him, loving him, making him feel better.

But that night, after we had all gone to bed, he woke me up with his coughing.

It was November 2015.

2. NOT JUST A DOG; NEVER 'JUST' A DOG

Besides Herbie, you're going to meet a few more interstellar hounds in these pages. I thought it would be nice for you to hear a little more about them.

Dirk

Dirk, passed away when he was 7 years old. He was a male deerhound much loved by Sarah. A stunning looking boy, he won prizes at shows. As part of a dog obedience team he appeared at Crufts dog show in a demonstration. He was a very clever boy as well as beautiful, and was a comical character who would regularly make Sarah roar with laughter.

Sarah loved Dirk because he was such a character, gentle and sweet, very clever, extremely handsome, and comical. Sarah did a lot of training with him and that strengthened their bond. Even with three other dogs, Dirk was special – everyone who met him would say the same.

Sara

Sara, a Bedlington whippet cross, was nearly 15 when she left us. She was owned and loved by Liz. She was a little monkey, and her young years were bit of a blur. She often ran off as lurchers do, but she always came back. She was part of the family and lovely, and Liz and Sarah really bonded once Sara had calmed down at about the age of 8. Liz was at home a lot, and they relied on each other's company. Sara was always there, and Liz's life revolved around her until she was gone.

She taught Liz to walk and talk and not stand still because Sara would get bored and run off. Thanks to Sara, Liz ended up walking early every morning, through the fields, seeing beautiful sunrises and all of nature that she would not have experienced without her. Later, in her old age, the farmer opened up the field on the other side of the oak trees so that Liz and Sara were able to walk under the oak trees through a little path and over to the other side. This was her new adventure and she would run with excitement, even though her legs were stiff with arthritis. She did this till the day her vestibular came on suddenly. Four days later she passed on.

Liz loved Sara because she was always there and she was such a gentle soul. She was always a friendly dog to everyone. Sara relied on Liz and Liz relied on Sara. Liz says, "After nearly 15 years they become part of you and the way you live your life."

Buttons

Buttons was a 7-month old female Bedlington Terrier owned and adored by Lynda. "Buttons was a beautiful, quiet, loving, always gentle dog who always wanted to be with us. I carried her most places because she did not have a lot of energy, but she did short walks. She always seemed a bit accident prone, would walk into toys, and sometimes the door. She was very black and kept her dark colour.

She was small, and when I took her to puppy training she didn't really want to get involved, would hide under the chair. I did continue with it but didn't take her to any follow on training, she copied Jasper (Lynda's other dog) so would sit, come when called, and she was toilet trained at an early age.

She seemed to feel the cold a lot, but in hindsight I know this was because she was ill. I often thought she couldn't see, but there was no evidence of this at the vet. Sadly, I always knew that something was not right.

After a tough personal period in Lynda's life, her husband agreed she could have a companion for Jasper, as something new to focus on. She says, "We chose Buttons because whenever anyone held her she would nibble at the buttons on your clothing. When she did it to our daughter she suggested the name. She was small, gentle, feminine, very pretty and cute. Very much wanted, and very much loved."

She had a personality like a baby, sleeping a lot, eating her food, toileting. She enjoyed play and walks in very short spurts. Lynda would carry her inside her jacket or jumper when she got tired, and she would look around taking it all in and sniffing in the air. She loved it! Lynda says, "If I put her down she would just sit and look as if to say, no thank you! Carry me! She was unable to walk far, carrying her became hard work so we used a cloth shopping bag with a blanket in the bottom, she loved it, was looking all around and getting lots of attention."

Sadly, her personality changed with her illness, she became irritable, restless, and wanted to be left alone.

Barney

Barney was a male Whippet x Bedlington who was fourteen when he passed away. He was owned and loved by Libby, who says, "I rescued Barney at 11 weeks old from the Blue Cross (January 2003). He was a stray but believed to be abandoned by local travellers. A scruffy little blonde lurcher who was all legs and fluff! Before he was allowed to be adopted the Blue Cross did a 'home check' – it was December and he came into the house, had a sniff, the cat looked him up and down, as if to say 'what's that!!?' and then Barney cocked his leg up the Christmas Tree – that was the only naughty thing he ever did in fourteen years.

"Barney was the kindest, wisest, most gorgeous dog with a beautiful soul. He was so in tune to my feelings and emotions, his love was unconditional and he would've taken a bullet for me, as I would for him. He never put a paw wrong, all he ever wanted was to please me, have a nice walk every day, a full bowl of food and water and a duvet to snuggle under every night. He never judged anyone and would always rest his head on the knee of anyone who was feeling low or unhappy, look to them with his big brown eyes and it just seemed to make everything alright. He was my best friend and soul mate.

"When I got my two whippets, he showed them the way to behave. He was like a grandad figure to them both and also to friend's puppies who spent many an hour with 'uncle Barney' showing them the ropes. He was also a cat loving Lurcher, quite rare I believe!

"All dogs are 'special' but every now and then a 'very

special' dog touches your life – Barney was one of these.

Poppy

Poppy was the much loved Bedlington cross Whippet belonging to Helen. Poppy was 12 and ¾ when she passed away. A total character, Poppy was strong, determined, feisty, and very loving. She adored her food, right up to an hour before she died. Having been a very naughty puppy, she turned into a well behaved young/older lady. She was very much loved by the whole family, and her nephew Bertie.

Helen loved Poppy for her determination and bravery, because even while suffering from a debilitating illness, she never complained and she never let things get her down. She remained loving, warm, and gentle. On the other hand, she was also feisty, barky and determined!

Diggs

Diggs was a male border terrier aged 13 or 14 when he passed away. He was the much loved and 'perfect' pet belonging to Heather. He was rescued as a companion for Heather's other dog Ralph, who was disabled from birth. Heather says, "It was love at first sight. Diggs was so laid back and happy. We could take him everywhere with us. He was happy just to be with us, you couldn't have a better companion. He was perfect in every way. He gave so much love to us and demanded nothing."

Diggs was a happy chap, friendly to everyone and other animals as well. He liked to be by Heather's side all day long and had 100% recall so Heather knew she could leave him off lead even in places like the woods. "He would stay by me." My husband loved Diggs but Diggs was my boy. He was my shadow, my soulmate. There have been many dogs during my life but there are a few that were special.

Diggs was very special."

3. WHEN YOU KNOW YOUR DOG IS GOING TO PASS AWAY

Crikey, this will be a hard chapter to write. And read. If you are going through a tough situation with your best friend right now, take a deep breath. Let's do it together.

Between Herbie starting to cough and me letting him go, there were seven months. These seven months were long on stress and worrying and fearing his loss, and extremely short on time to pack a lifetime of love into. I was painfully aware that being without him for the rest of my life would never stop hurting.

Initially I was puzzled by the cough. I rang the vet the very next day and they told me not to worry, it was probably an after-effect of the general anaesthetic. But he was still coughing 48 hours later and I was worried, so I took him back down to see them.

I should say at this stage that my vet, Sandra, is fantastic and I have total faith in her. Over the next few weeks Herbie had some tests. These showed his kidneys weren't functioning brilliantly, but nothing serious. They also showed he had a heart murmur. Nothing really to worry about. Many dogs have heart murmurs and live happily for years. Sandra gave us some tablets, and the cough began to settle. It didn't completely stop though, and over the next weeks and months I was a regular at the surgery. He would improve for a while and then it would get worse so I'd take him back. Sandra was trying to find a happy medium between heart and kidney medication. Apart from the cough, Herbie was his normal happy self. Racing and shouting and eating and having a riot - as always.

But I was becoming increasingly uneasy.

In February he had an 'episode'. That's all I can describe it as. He seemed too warm, was breathing quite shallowly, and then appeared to collapse. He couldn't get his breath. It was late in the evening and I wanted to call Sandra, but my husband said to call in the morning. But in the morning Herbie was fine.

A few weeks later I glanced over at him and did a double take. Herbie was in his basket and seemed to have a hitch when he breathed in. It wasn't all the time. It was a kind of twitch. I told the vet about it and she wasn't happy, but she couldn't find anything else wrong with him. By now it was April and my anxiety was increasing. I was frightened. I knew something was really wrong.

Looking back now I see photos of him from November 2015 onwards and I think, "well he looked thin. Why didn't I notice? Why wasn't it obvious to me he was ill?" But it wasn't. Herbie was always a skinny, delicate dog. He maintained his weight throughout his illness (although we found out eventually that this was due to fluid retention). But looking back, I still can't believe I couldn't see just how poorly he was.

It is one of the things we do when we lose our best friend, we channel the guilt. "Why didn't I see?" "If only I had seen." I know it is something you'll be experiencing too. I can tell you that you have done - or are doing - all that you could, and I can tell you not to beat yourself up about it. But I know that I felt responsible, that even now, I still feel like I let him down. I was his number one. I should have done better.

This sense that something wasn't right, and the concern I had about his cough went on for what felt like a lifetime, until one terrible day when I noticed the skin around his throat was loose, and when I touched it I realised it was a build-up of fluid in his chest and throat. I can't describe the horrendous lurch I had at that moment, the scream in my head. I was beside myself and was on the phone straight away. I reached the locum vet. I wanted Sandra but she was unavailable, and I knew Herbie had to be seen straightaway, so I took him in. The locum was sweet, kind, and then she said something that chilled me to the bone. "It's just a case of giving him the best life you can now."

It was stark, and while not entirely unexpected, it was such an awful shock I just went to pieces. I managed to stutter out, "How long?" and she shrugged and looked sad. Then she asked me if I was alright.

No, of course I wasn't alright. She was sympathetic, but professional. Meanwhile my world had just torn itself asunder.

When my husband came home that night I collapsed on his shoulder, and later I cried myself to sleep. That was the start of many tearful nights, and extreme anxiety. I needed to find ways to get through the weeks ahead. I practiced a lot of deep breathing. I let myself cry when I needed to. I stroked Herbie's head a lot. I wrote a little because I found it therapeutic.

You'll find some of those pieces in this book.

What about other owners who knew they were going to lose their best friends?

Sarah knew for a long time that Dirk, her 7-year old deerhound was poorly. He was diagnosed at five years with heart disease and auto-immune deficiency so she knew he was running out of time. When she heard he was terminal she says she was devastated because he was so young. "He was still appearing perfectly healthy at the time and it seemed impossible. I also felt angry and decided that I wouldn't have any more pedigree deerhounds after him, because it is too sad to deal with. I also felt a bit angry that breeders and the breed club are not doing enough to combat this problem in the breed."

Libby knew she was going to lose Barney, but thought she would have longer than she did. She recognised that Barney at 14 was 'a good age', and that he had been lucky to have a wonderful life since she had adopted him, but then, "devastation took over and I started clutching at straws to see if there was anything else that could be done – basically panic set in."

Libby tried to take every day as it came, enjoying every walk, every cuddle, and every moment with Barney while trying to keep life as normal as possible, she says, "so as not to alert him that something was up."

Helen too was devastated, knowing she was going to lose Poppy, and was unsure how she would cope. She says, "because Poppy went blind in the final six months of her life, it ripped the heart out of me watching her struggle to find her way and bumping into things. Especially her struggle to climb the stairs, and come down again on the day I lost her. It made me very, very sad."

4. A LETTER FROM HERBIE

As I said, while Herbie was poorly I managed to carry on with some of my writing. One of the things I wrote at the time was a letter *from* Herbie *to* me. He was in his basket beside me, under my desk. I found myself wondering what he would say to me if he could. This is the letter that we wrote together.

DEAR MUM

You are as beloved to me as I am to you. I'm watching you as your heart breaks and I think you have more pain than me. I want to talk to you about my life. Today you think you received the second worst news about me that is possible, and you know that the worst is not very far away. So I wanted to write this now while we are still physically together, because when I'm gone, the pain will be too much for you, and I know you, you will have your doubts.

You have given me everything I have ever possibly wanted and so much more besides. I have had the best food, the best care, fresh water, a warm, soft bed and so much love. So, so, so much love that it burst out of you – every pore and fibre.

How I adore your touch. The way you stroke me. You know all my curves, and all my sharp points. You know how every inch of me feels. You bury your face in my neck. You kiss my belly. You hold my paws. You scruggle my ears. You'll miss that, I know.

Remember the first day you saw me? I was pretty independent even at four weeks. I've always had a mind of my own. I was blue. You nearly didn't choose me because your other dog had

25

been blue. So you thought about having my black brother, but something changed your mind. I like to think it was my charm and good looks. I was 'Sooty' then but you changed my name to Herbie. The day you got a phone call to say I was ready, I was just 7 weeks old. A few days later, I came home from rural Lincolnshire with you. We sat in the back of the car and bonded while Dad drove. You became my Mum on that long trip home. I didn't even cry to be away from my canine Mum. I was ready for new adventures. You were mine and I was yours and that was that.

You're typing this for me one handed while stroking my head and scruggling behind my ears. It feels nice. It always has. It's a comfort.

You're scared. You're scared because you know the concept of 'future'. I don't though. I live entirely in the present. You are afraid, because you want to do what is right, but you know how much pain it will cause you. I know I can trust you to put me first though, Mum, always. Because you always have.

You think your heart will stop when mine does? It won't. It may pause for what seems an interminable amount of time while you accept I'm gone, and then it will go on beating, and I will walk within you, in every moment, until you too cease to exist. Maybe we'll walk together then. I hope so.

You worry that people will think you foolish when you break down, when you can't breathe through the tears? When you shake and when you forget things. Don't be. The ones that love you, the ones that love their own animals, the good ones – they will understand and they will carry us both in their hearts.

You have always seen the good in me, seldom been cross, never raised your voice to me or touched me with anything but adoration. You loved our training classes. You were so proud of all my achievements – especially my amazing recall. Top of the class! You always secretly loved my cheekiness, my bossiness, my demands.

You and I have understood everything that passed between us – every tip of the head, every smile, every click of the tongue, every look and meaningful exchange. You knew me better than you knew yourself. You loved my intelligence and talked to me all the time. I really loved that, Mum.

I've had so many good times! I have loved my life! It was so much fun! It was noisy and smelly and interesting and crazy. All those squirrels and cats! All those bushes to sniff. Fun chases with my sister, Satin. Exploring with little Betsy. All those interesting titbits you gave me to eat. All my lovely walks with my wonderful Daddy. I loved Northumberland when I was an 'only' dog and I loved all the open spaces and the sandy beaches where I ran in huge, looping circles. That's the lurcher in me, isn't it Mum?

And I loved the quiet times, when we snuggled on the couch, or when I sat on your feet as you worked in your study. Or the times we had the bed to ourselves and I lay against Dad's pillow and you slept with your hand on my bum. That was nice. I loved the cross armed Herbie cuddle, being enveloped in your arms, our special hug, with me standing on your foot. Always remember me that way, Mum.

I'm sorry we didn't get longer together. You wanted to take me into my grizzly, grumpy old age, but I guess my heart is a bit worn out from all that love we shared.

Remember me as I was. Alert and handsome and intelligent and fun and communicative. Remember how fast I was. And how clumsy. Remember me with tears and laughter. Remember me though it hurts to do so, because the pain you have is equal to the love we shared, and as long as you feel something, I am here with you. There is no goodbye if you carry me in your heart. Remember all the joy, Mum, because there was so much of it for both of us.

Thank you for looking after me now, your constant reassurances, your hand soft on my head. I see you searching my face, needing to know. I'll let you know, Mum. And it will be the right thing to do, for me. If it's right for me, it's right for you.

And remember – you are as beloved to me as I am to you. I know I am loved – know I loved you too.

Eternally yours

Herbie Longfellow Alderdice

Did writing that letter help me?

Who knows, perhaps it did on the day I wrote it. I posted it on Facebook so that my friends would know what I was going through and support me if they felt they could (and some did). However, since that day I have never read the letter again. I have just pasted it into this manuscript without reading it. I will read it when I come to the editing stage, and I'll cry buckets.

(Edited to say, I did).

I've always known the letter existed even though I haven't been able to remember the content, and do you know, strangely there is some solace. It's a love letter from my dog to me that I wrote while he was in arm's reach and I know that is what he would have said to me.

Maybe, if you still have time, you can write one from your dog to yourself? What would your dog say to you if they could talk?

5. WHAT SHOULD YOU DO WHEN YOU KNOW YOUR DOG IS TERMINALLY ILL?

When you know your dog is terminally ill, there is no denying you will have a traumatic time. You may decide to let your best friend go very quickly (as Lynda did with Buttons) or you may be able to spend more time with your dog without a totally diminished quality of life (as Sarah did with Dirk).

In my case, Sandra called me back in as soon as she heard the news I'd received about Herbie from the locum. I expect the veterinary nurse, the lovely Hayley, told her how upset I had been in the surgery. Sandra assured me she would do everything she could, and that Herbie could stay with me while he still had a good quality of life and was happy. She told me not to give up just yet.

So what advice would I give you if you find out your dog is terminally ill? The first thing you should do is check that you have all the information you need about your dog's illness. If there is any chance your vet could be wrong, you may well want a second opinion. In my case it was the locum who told me Herbie was terminally ill, and it was confirmed by Sandra, but Sandra then did everything she could to extend his life while balancing the quality of life he was experiencing. That leads to my second point.

At no stage of your dog's final illness should any of this become about **you** or another member of the family. The

31

quality of your dog's life is paramount. I know you're reading this book because of how much you love your best friend. In the immortal words of Sting, and yes, I suppose it has become a cliché, "If you love someone, set them free."

Pain can be managed to an extent, and our veterinary nurse told me that animals process the feelings of pain differently to humans, but if you have any suspicions that your friend is hurting or feeling pain or severe discomfort, let them go.

I can't emphasize that enough.

How soon is too soon?

Oh this is a horrible quandary. My husband and I were at odds about this. He would say, "We'll wait, we'll see," but I had the screaming habdabs about leaving it too long, while at the same time, selfishly wanting Herbie to stay with me forever.

My veterinary nurse said to me, "You'll know when the time is right," and that's true. I remember the moment Toby told me he'd had enough very clearly. We were out walking, and he stopped. That was it. I had to carry him home.

For months after Herbie had passed, I figured he hadn't told me, he had seemed so intent on soldiering on. I now see that on that final morning when I woke up and saw him standing there, having not slept all night, well that was a megaphone announcement, wasn't it? He was uncomfortable and unhappy. I loved him, he loved me. I had to make the decision.

He had a routine appointment that day anyway, and when I told my vet he probably hadn't slept she looked me straight in the eye and I nodded and wept. We understood that that day, 29th July, was the day.

I understand that you don't want to rob your dog of a moment of life, and it may be that you can hang on a few hours, or a few days, but make sure you're extending life for the right reasons, and not holding off the finality of the end, and your own pain. You love your best friend, so put them first.

There are many stories (with photos) on the internet of people giving their dogs a great last day and having the appointment at the end of the afternoon. That way you get to make some more extra special memories to cherish forever. My favourite was one from 12th November 2016, when Mark Woods asked people to join him on Porth beach in Newquay, Cornwall, UK for a last walk with his greyhound, Walnut. Hundreds of dogs and their owners turned up in a fitting tribute to a wonderful and loving companion. I watched on a webcam and needless to say, cried buckets.

Try and live in the moment

Hahaha!

This is a case of do as I say and not as I do. Believe me, I had seven weeks to love Herbie enough to last a lifetime, and I think I did a pretty good job of that. However, my anxiety levels were through the roof. I was desperately afraid for him, and for myself. I was scared of the amount of pain he might have; I was scared of not being strong enough to cope. I was embarrassed about what others thought about me constantly weeping and worrying about my boy. I was terrified each day was his last. I dreaded going to work and leaving him (someone was always with him in those last weeks – in fact on one memorable day, my Mum and Dad came a long way just to dog sit), and I hated heading home to see how he was and facing up to it. I was desperately afraid of being left alone in this world when he finally went.

But I did touch him and cuddle him and walk with him and love him, every single moment I could. Towards the end I cooked him special meals and in the last few days I hand fed him. I did cherish those moments, especially being able to tell him how much I loved him - over and over and over again.

Tips on preparing yourself for the end

Be prepared

You know the end is coming so there is no excuse. Have your vet's number programmed into your phone for the moment you need it. Know how to contact her after hours. Make sure there is always petrol in the car or you know the number for a taxi service or a friend. Try and prepare yourself emotionally and mentally – easier said than done.

Ensure your dog is comfortable

Sarah, owner of Dirk, remembers that in the run up to the end she "just knew I had to make him comfortable and keep his quality of life as good as possible, up until the last minute. I am satisfied I did that, which has been the only comfort."

I feel the same way about Herbie. I did everything I could to make him feel comfortable, and know he was loved. This what he told his Facebook fans on his page on 13th July 2016 (please excuse his colloquial use of speech):

> *Hello everyone I'm still here. Bit sleepy, you know? But my koff is better on the steroids. Mum keeps weeping over me so I gets wet but other than that, life's ok. I am having the most amazing retirement. Little walks where I want to go. Any dinner I want in small measures - so scrambled egg and sardines are my favourite. Last night I had rice, potato and lamb gravy. I am fussed and petted all the time and never left on my own. Everyone is very gentle with me. I have wees whenever I want and my water is always being freshened up, and I have as many marrowbone biscuits as I want - I've given up on bonios - too hard. I sleep on the big bed ALL night. I love it.*
>
> *Back to the vet tomorrow to have a check-up.*
>
> *Wuvs to you all and be kind to each other xxxx*

That was his last post, but it makes me smile. He was poorly, but okay.

Communicate

Be open and honest with your vet about your dog and their symptoms. Ask for time frames (you probably won't get any definitive answers). Try and understand what possible side-effects of any drugs your dog is taking, will be.

Talk to your partner and family – they have a right to know as much as you do. Maybe they will be some comfort to you. I hope so.

It is also worth having a conversation with your boss or colleagues if you are likely to need time away from work. If they know what you are going through they should be quite sympathetic to your needs.

Talk to your dog – s/he needs you as much as you need them.

Start thinking about what you will do when the time comes.

Will you cremate or bury your pet? Will you bury your best friend in the garden or a pet cemetery? Will you send your best friend to a crematorium via your vet or will you arrange this yourself? Find out costs and locations, and deal with the practicalities now. There's no funeral director to help you, as there would be with a human relative, unless you're prepared to pay plenty of money for the privilege of a 'specialist'.

My veterinary nurse spoke to me a few weeks before Herbie passed about cremation and told me they had a cheaper option whereby your pet was cremated along with a number of others and then the ashes scattered in the memorial garden of the crematorium. At the time I was quite shocked, so I was ready on the day to say, "Hell, no," but cometh the hour, Sandra said - without even consulting me - "private cremation and ashes returned in a casket" - which was a relief! She knew what I needed.

Remember, forewarned is forearmed. If you know there will be options, and some of these may distress you, sort them out beforehand.

There are probably other things you should do when you know you will lose your best friend imminently, but you won't have the energy reserves to deal with everything. Knowing you are going to lose him or her, at a set time, with the help of your vet, in a few days or weeks is horrendous. It's an anxious waiting game.

Take heart though. Can it really be any worse than the shock of them collapsing in your arms suddenly? At least those of us who are given time, get to say our goodbyes.

Pre-grief: Yes, it is a 'thing'

Dealing with your best friend's terminal illness is tough, and you'll start to grieve as soon as you know you're coming to the end. It's torturous, watching and anticipating every little change, feeling those waves of sorrow, wishing you could hold back time or at least pause it. I found those final few weeks so incredibly difficult. I wanted to be with Herbie, but I wanted to escape the horrendous pain of impending loss. Part of me wanted it to be over, and part of me wanted it never to finish, because at the end of the day, at least my agony about his illness meant he was still alive. It was a pitiful quandary, and while I never want to feel that way again, if we could turn back time and those last few weeks were all I was offered, I'd go right back there, and cuddle his head once more.

I for one am thankful I had the time to say goodbye. I had a few weeks. It took me all that time to tell Herbie the extent of my love. It took me all that time to cram in the love that I needed to give him, the love that I knew would have to last me the rest of my time on earth. I will cherish that love in all the time I have remaining to me – throughout my life without him.

6. IF EUTHANASIA IS NEW TO YOU: PERSONAL EXPERIENCES

If you have never been present when a pet has been put to sleep before, it may help you to read about some personal experiences.

I was glad that I had been there for Toby when he was euthanized ten years previously. I felt I knew what was going to happen to Herbie, and that took some of the fear away.

With Toby, my vet discussed a casket before the event, and I think I actually paid up front too. That was pretty awful. My husband was with me (we were newly married) and so he was a source of strength for me. Toby lay on the table and the vet shaved a section of Toby's fur. I held him and I spoke to him through the whole process. I wanted my voice to be the last he heard. The vet injected him. It was quick and he became floppy very quickly. He didn't close his eyes. I cuddled him and kept on speaking to him. I asked the vet if Toby was gone and she listened for a heartbeat and nodded.

I stayed a little while and he made lots of strange stomach noises and at one stage twitched. I remember thinking, "He's alive!" and being momentarily overjoyed, until I realised that even if he was, I would have to do it all again. He was far too poorly to be magically alright. I found this emotional rollercoaster incredibly traumatic, and it haunts me to this day.

So, it was with the awareness of Toby's experience that I

approached Herbie's passing with some trepidation.

Herbie was well known to Sandra and as you have seen, she had done everything to keep him comfortable and help him survive in the previous six months. I'd been a regular visitor to the surgery, sometimes several times a week, and so Sandra knew both my husband and I well. To be fair, she is probably equally as wonderful and gracious with all of her patients and their parents, I don't think Herbie and I were special! The two veterinary nurses, Hayley and Elaine, were fabulous too. I say this, because it made a huge difference.

On that final day, we had an 8.45 am appointment and surgery was running a little late. Herbie and I drove in, and John followed me down in his own car because he was going on afterwards to work. He was held up by cows at a crossing – the joys of living in The Land of Clouds and Forest. Sandra did the usual checks on Herbie, and John arrived just as Sandra and I were discussing Herbie's lack of sleep. At the moment that I decided to do what I imagined was right, I felt very keenly that John wanted to wait, but as Sandra said, if we put it off, it could only be for a few hours. It just wasn't fair.

She recommended we go out with Herbie and wait until the end of surgery. We sat on a blanket on the steps in the car park. It was raining. One of the nurses brought us a coffee each. I cried completely unashamedly as people came and went. I'm sure as pet owners themselves they fully sympathised with our situation. We petted Herbie and talked to him. I kept telling him what a good boy he was and how proud I was.

When all the other patients had gone we returned to the consulting room and Sandra talked us through what would happen. She told me it was basically an overdose of anaesthesia and he would fall asleep and then his heart would stop. He wouldn't know anything. She told me not to expect his eyes to close as dogs don't have eyelids that work in the same way as us humans'. She also told me that after he died, he might make strange noises, or jerk, and this was completely normal. It was such a relief to hear this, as Toby's death had left me quite shaken.

Then Sandra and I discussed how to do it. Herbie couldn't lie down comfortably and I didn't want him to be uncomfortable at all, therefore forcing him to sit or lie down was out of the question. We decided he would be standing and we would hold him up. Herbie was always a leaner. He would lean in to me whenever Sandra tried to listen to his lungs and his heart. It was amusing. She would complain to him that she could hear my heart and not his! I'd have to gently push him up and away from me so she could listen to what was happening to him. Understanding this leaning tendency meant that holding Herbie up was a straightforward solution.

To my eternal regret I took the rear side, and my husband took the front end next to me to support his head. I should have taken his head, but it all happened very quickly and we were in position, not really by choice. One of the nurses had his back end, and the other had the other side. So we supported him between us. He was as light as a feather anyway. I used to say he had bird bones.

Again it was very quick. I was talking to him the most, but

we all spoke to him. Sandra bade him goodbye and told him he had been a wonderful brave boy, and I kissed my gentle lad over and over and told him what a good boy he was and how lucky I was.

I think as the needle went in, and Sandra said 'here we go, Herbie', my heart stopped beating, seemed to pause and hold on indefinitely for a while. In my mind I was screaming, 'no, no, no' but the sensible rational grown up part of me just got on with it. I hate that element of me. I will always remember the feeling of him relaxing in my arms until he was no weight at all.

And we lay him down … and I breathed out … and my heart started beating again.

But Herbie's didn't. Sandra checked him thoroughly and told me Herbie had gone. Herbie had passed away, at my instigation, and I was alone in the world without him. My greatest fear.

We were allowed to stay with him for quite a long time, and I wept and wept. I'm crying again now just remembering. You'll know all about that terrible feeling of loss, I know and I sympathise.

He didn't make any noise or move at all. His eyes were closed most of the way. I'm happy about all of this, because Toby had given me such a start, and I recognised that with Herbie, I had to accept the reality of the situation as quickly as possible or I would go mad.

Sandra shaved some of Herbie's fur off for me and placed it in an envelope. I took his collar and lead. I sat there for a long time, holding his white paw (he had one white front paw, the others were grey). I stroked him and smoothed him. I cried. I wailed. I told him I loved him and how much I would miss him. Eventually I could feel that his body was starting to cool down, so I had to say my final goodbye. It was horrible. I held on to that paw till the last moment.

In my mind, I'm still holding it.

* * *

Thank heavens for decent and kind vets. Sandra was brilliant, and Lynda had a good one too. She notes that her referral vet was amazing when she lost Buttons. "He gave us so much time, and was so reassuring that the decision we made was the right one. There was no hurry to leave. The vet carried her to the car for me and put her in so gently, he seemed so caring and genuinely sorry." Lynda also had a lovely phone call from her local vet who spent a long time talking through what had happened and again reassured Lynda that she had made the right decision. "They were always there for me," she remembers.

Sandra advised John and I to take it easy as we would have headaches all day and that we shouldn't drive. John had to go to work, and he says that he spent the whole day feeling numb and worrying about me. I drove to a supermarket car park and tried to recover some strength. I then went in and bought a few things, but I remember standing at the checkout having a conversation with the operator in a normal voice wondering how that was possible. "I just said goodbye to my best friend!" was the thought that was shrieking over and over in my mind. I wondered if I looked like I'd just been breaking my heart. I'm a messy crier. The checkout operator didn't mention anything, thank goodness!

I drove back to our house in The Land of Clouds and Forest, about twenty minutes away, and then once inside my front door, I let the floodgates open once more. Herbie wouldn't be coming home with me ever again. I cried on and off all day. I managed to ring my Mum and we cried together.

Many people express their relief that their dog's suffering is over, and I had an element of that. I had so wanted Herbie to live, but the guilt that he might have been in pain was killing me. Liz experienced this too, and says, "I knew what I had to do. It was a relief and I knew it was the right thing to do. It all went so well. The vet came to the house and I held Sara who simply couldn't be bothered as she was so tired. She went so peacefully for which I am so grateful."

7. INITIAL GRIEF

How do you describe what the initial sensation of grief feels like? I personally was at once numbed, and at the same time I felt as though every cell in my body was on fire. How can that be?

And I so wanted Herbie's death not to be true, not to have happened, even though letting Herbie go was my decision, and mine alone. For the first few days, I held on to every passing moment, thinking, 'he was just here, he was here with me' as though I could cling on to his existence merely by ensuring he felt real, that he wasn't a figment of my imagination.

I desperately clung on to his nearness – 'he was here today', 'he was here just 24 hours ago', 'it was just 48 hours', 'he was here with me this week'.

I'm not sure that will make sense to anyone else. Perhaps it does. We all have our quirks and oddities where our best friends are concerned.

But that's the point of this book really. I can't tell you how it will be for you, because everybody experiences grief differently. It is a journey we make mostly on our own, and our beliefs and experiences colour the journey.

Let's look at some other people's experiences. Maybe these are similar to your feelings?

***

For Lynda, the decision to have Buttons put to sleep was sudden and heart breaking. She says, "It was all completely surreal, I felt as if I was on the outside watching someone else go through it. We had been referred as an emergency to a centre on the opposite side of the country for a scan, and possible surgery. When we saw the scan we were offered brain surgery or to have her put to sleep. I had knowledge about her (now diagnosed) condition, and what surgery involved and made the decision to have her put to sleep. At this point she was still anaesthetised in the scanner, and we were offered to wake her up so we could say goodbye or do it while she was still anaesthetised. We chose the second option which we believed was kindest to her, so the next time we saw her she had died."

Lynda says, "I was heartbroken. The vet carried her out and very gently gave her to me, she looked like my sleeping baby, but at peace. I held her in my arms and felt so numb, I don't think I even cried at that point. My husband was crying. Part of me was relieved, and then I felt guilty for those thoughts. We were hundreds of miles away from home. The last thing my daughter said to me was that she had a feeling she wouldn't see her again once we took her there, so that was going through my head too. Then I was feeling 'what now?' In reality I was totally shocked, and could not believe it. I had people to tell which was really hard. It was like being two people, factual and practical, then bawling my eyes out. I felt helpless and really vulnerable."

For Sarah, losing young Dirk was expected and yet sudden at the end too. "He was poorly, but he had been poorly for some time – I took him to the vet in the car at about 10pm at night, when we arrived and opened the car, he was dead. He had obviously died peacefully on the way. I was very shocked, then heartbroken to think I hadn't said goodbye properly."

Like Lynda, Sarah notes that she experienced some relief it was over, "because having a very sick dog is very stressful particularly when I work away from home and was always worrying about him. His treatment was also bankrupting me, although I was happy to spend everything I earned on him. Sometimes one does wonder how much longer you can carry on. Obviously this goes along with sadness and missing him a lot."

Liz came home to be greeted as normal by fifteen-year old Sara, but then Sara suddenly started walking in circles. She had vestibular. The vet expected Sara to be fine in a few days, but although she responded to initial treatment and seemed happy, with a waggy tail, on the fourth day Liz could see she wasn't right. "I knew her time was up and that she had shut down."

Liz says, "Thinking Sara would hopefully get better, it was a shock when I realised Monday morning that I would need to make a decision. By mid-morning I phoned the vets because I could not bear to see her unhappy. I felt it almost a practical decision that was taken out of my hands as I could not let her suffer. I knew this time would come and I had also been worried about how we would cope in the long term as she needed 24-hour supervision. I do not mean this from a selfish point of view. Far from it. Eventually one needs to leave the house etc. and I couldn't bear the thought of her being left alone or stumbling and hurting herself. As she would not take any food and was very weak and on the Monday wouldn't sleep, just lay hunched up.

"Initially, after lots of tears, there was almost a high. One of relief it had gone so well, and one of relief she wasn't suffering. We even watched a video of when she was young. Little did I know how much it would hit me the next day and actually the next five months and more. No more walks and reasons to get up early. No company when I sat down to have my sandwich at lunchtime. No company in the evening if I was on my own. No dog lying beside my bed at night time. No need to cook chicken and rice of which the cat missed his share. Seeing other people walk their dogs made me feel sad and I wanted to tell them to appreciate every moment they have and to realise how lucky they are and I realised too that I had taken for granted the blessing that I had a truly wonderful friend."

Helen too says, "Although I hate to admit this, I was relieved that Poppy did not have to struggle any more. I was relieved that I did not have to watch her struggle, but after that, I broke down and felt totally lost without her."

Diggs had become pretty poorly, and Heather remembers, "He got up to go to the door in the early hours and he fell. I jumped up to lift him and he looked at me with such a beautiful face and a gentle wag of his tail. My husband suggested we ring the vets and get some different tablets, but I could see Diggs wanted to go. The life had gone from his eyes, and his body was limp. We drove to the vet with him cuddled in his blanket and our hearts breaking. I had tears pouring down my cheeks. His eyes were closed and he had laboured breathing. I was still hoping the vet would say something could be done, but we could see nothing could.

"We stayed with him after the injection and I sung to him silly songs I had made up for him over the ten years we had loved and lived with him. I could hardly breathe when I saw he had gone. On one hand I wanted to bring him back and on the other I was relieved his suffering was over.

"We drove back, his little head still warm on my chest and me still singing to him. When we got back I just looked at my husband and shook my head. I couldn't believe he had gone. I couldn't believe we couldn't have saved him. We took him up to lay him on our bed while my husband dug his grave. We took our other boy Ronnie to see him and say goodbye."

Heather had a very physical reaction to the loss of Diggs. "I felt sick, my heart was banging, I was shivering. There was a real aching coldness in my chest. I felt like I was going to burst with grief. I didn't think I could cope. I couldn't stand. I took several painkillers and drunk wine. I became drunk. I sat watching TV without seeing it."

Lynda also had a physical reaction. "I could not stop crying, I felt ill, really wretched, and I had a dull pain in my chest. I felt sick and couldn't be bothered to eat. On days I was not working I couldn't even be bothered to wash and dress. I would just cuddle Jasper and cry. He spent weeks looking for her, sniffing at doors, looking generally lost. At times I was just numb and would sit staring into space. I was totally shocked. I would go over it endlessly in my mind, and then tell my husband and upset him. I felt so sad, and very guilty. I don't think I have ever stopped grieving, I think about her often. I still when I feel low, occasionally wonder if I made the right decision. I still have times when I sit and cry, or I will be unable to sleep and it will be in my head."

After Dirk had gone, Sarah remembers she had a generally heavy heart, "particularly when going to or past his old favourite places. I was a bit depressed as I always am as I love my dogs and it depresses me how short their lives are. I stopped sleeping for a while worrying about whether we could have done anything else for him, and hoping he wasn't in pain or distressed when he actually died. I'm convinced now that we couldn't have done much more for him."

Libby remembers, "I probably had two weeks of crying for most of the day. I dreamt of him most nights for a least the first month. I felt a pain in my stomach and felt very sick for at least three weeks and the mention of his name would just create a sadness in me that I can't really put into words."

Helen was very tearful and sad too. "For the first week I cried every day for her, I could not eat very well, I could not sleep very well, and in the morning automatically looked for her beside my bed. Even though I knew it was the right thing to do, to let her go, I felt guilt, could I have done more, if I had more money could I have saved her? Six weeks later, I still have overwhelming grief, and can cry at any time (like now writing this)."

What you feel is normal for you

What these shared experiences have shown us is that there are some common occurrences on the loss of our dogs. The feelings of devastation and of relief are shared almost universally. We may have difficulty owning up to some of our feelings, but deep down, they seem to be common among everyone.

Devastation – it's awful.

It is not that you feel as though the world has ended, more that you wish it would. Or, with every death I have ever had experience of, I find myself wondering how it is that the world moves on as though nothing has changed, everything is normal.

 In your own life, something huge has happened, something fundamental and crippling. But all around you, life continues much as it ever has and people barely acknowledge this rift in the fabric of your life.

You will likely feel one or more of these emotions:

- Confused and disoriented
- Exhausted
- Overwhelmed
- Shocked
- Numb
- Fearful
- You may have physical symptoms: such as aches, headache, sore throat, nausea etc.

Grief is exhausting. Hiding grief from other people even more so. For some reason, so many of us feel a sense of shame when we break down after our dogs die. In the first few days, people are sympathetic, but because there is no expectation of a funeral and a long-term mourning process with animals as there is with humans, people tend to forget our misery quite quickly. So what do we, the bereaved do? We put a good face on and pretend we're alright. We get on with life.

I'm not saying this is the wrong thing to do. In many ways it is the right thing to do – not to dwell. But if you do want to acknowledge that you are still in pain, by all means do so. You are acknowledging your humanity and compassion, and you are completely worthy of further sympathy for your loss. As time goes by, you may need to be less open about it. All I'm suggesting is that if you wish to vocalise your sadness, do so.

I'm not a psychologist and I'm not one for psychobabble, so I'm not going to pretend to be an expert here, but there are a few things worth jotting down and including in this book so that you can choose to look at them, or not. Perhaps this will help you understand what happens when you are grieving.

* * *

The five stages of grief – by Elisabeth Kubler-Ross

In 1969 Elisabeth Kübler-Ross identified five stages of loss in her book On Death and Dying. These were:

- Denial and isolation

- Anger

- Bargaining

- Depression

- Acceptance

Kübler-Ross said that while we as individuals do not necessarily go through the stages in the same order, the stages of grief are universal and will all be experienced by people in relation to the deaths of loved ones, as well as relationship breakdowns and our own terminal illnesses.

I think what is useful about the Kübler-Ross model, is that each of the five stages should be seen as a tool kit that can help us understand what we're going through. We can apply her theory of grief to our own specific loss. Each stage is one aspect of grief. In some cases, these aspects of grief will co-exist together for long periods of time. In my case I recognise that I had a lot of anger and depression, co-existing for several months after Herbie's loss.

As individuals we will spend greater or lesser amounts of time at each stage, and our feelings may be intense at some moments, and not so intense at others. Theoretically, working through the stages, and by extension understanding what these stages are, can help us to peacefully accept our loss.

I can apply this to myself to give you an example.

1. Denial

My sense of denial came when I heard that Herbie was terminally ill. It could not be happening. In fact, I was probably in denial from the moment I first heard him cough in November 2015. I continued to be in denial for about thirty minutes or so after he had passed. Then I sat in my car and the sense of sadness that settled deep into my heart has stayed there ever since.

Denial before the event, may lead us avoid vet appointments, or to put them off. It means we don't hear what the vet is trying to tell us. We can't face up to the reality of the situation. It is an instinctive defence mechanism on our part. We try to hide away from reality.

But denial also helps us to continue living life after our loss. In spite of everything seeming meaningless and overwhelming, in spite of nothing making sense, we go on. We do the things we're supposed to and get through the day. We carry on breathing. My heart began to beat again, even though I didn't want it to.

Denial and shock, in the aftermath of a loss, are actually very useful. It means we take care of ourselves. We slow down, we only do what we can handle (and that might not be very much). This numbness we feel makes our own survival possible. It's clever. Once you start to accept the reality of your friend's loss you begin the healing process. As you become stronger, denial fades. Unfortunately, as denial fades, you start to feel more pain.

Denial after the event can be us trying to hang on to the friend that we loved so much. How long that lasts will be up to you. I know many dog owners who say, "I can't believe my dog's gone."

I can't either. But the reality is, he has.

2. Anger

Denial and isolation may begin to wear off and then perhaps you'll be angry. I didn't think I was angry. Who could I be angry at? Certainly not Herbie! And not my vet, because she did so much for him. That left myself, and I was just too sad to be angry at me, so I chose to be angry at the world and my poor husband. We were moving house yet again, and it was stressful anyway, but my emotion had to go somewhere and I directed it his way – for not understanding me, for not grieving as much as I was, for not caring. It was unfair, but it is a normal reaction.

You may well direct it inwards at yourself, or at your children, parents, another pet or a loved one. Perhaps you'll be angry at your boss or colleagues. Or at the supermarket checkout girl. It is horrible. You may not recognise yourself. You know of course, rationally, that no-one else is to blame, but you're in pain and you want to lash out. Knowing that you're doing this will make you feel angrier and sadder.

You'll also feel guilty. Guilty because of your pet's death and not being able to 'save' them (even from a grand old age). Guilty for lashing out at other people. And of course this guilt can make you angry once more, and then you will feel sad again.

And you're probably feeling really lonely too. This will mean you feel isolated again. These stages of grief are cyclical. There is no limit to the amount of pain you will feel, nor the depth of your pain, or the amount of time it will last.

Never deny your anger. We are trained from an early age not to express our anger, and so we tend to suppress it. Remember though that anger is another indication of the intensity of your love for your best friend. Don't feel guilty for being angry or upset.

However, do try to recognise it for what it is, and work through it. Ask for acceptance and understanding from your loved ones. You deserve it, and if they love you, of course they will forgive you.

3. Bargaining

When I knew I was going to lose Herbie I bargained. Boy did I bargain. I don't have a regular faith so in my case I was trying to ask the Universe to perform some sort of miracle. But mainly I prayed for strength for myself to let him go before he suffered, and that his passing would be calm and peaceful. I was scared to death he would be panicked or in pain.

I think the Universe granted my wishes and I am eternally grateful.

I didn't bargain after he had gone, perhaps because the

things I had wished for had come to pass, and I understood that the pain I was in, was mine to bear. Herbie was past all pain and that was the main thing.

In any case you may feel helpless and vulnerable.

You may plead for the clock to be turned back, or for it all to be a mistake. You may berate yourself for not seeking assistance sooner, or for not getting a second opinion. You will be full of doubts. You will feel guilty. You will beg for this not to have happened. You may want to make a deal with your God.

Go ahead. It's OK. It is normal. Everyone who reads this book sends you a hug. All of us know what you're going through, and we love you for loving your furry friend.

4. Depression

Oh my days.

Since I lost Herbie I haven't had a day where I didn't cry for him. I have what I call 'Herbie days'. These are days when I miss him so badly that I am weepy and depressed all day. On other days (actually most days even after twelve months), I will think of him, or a memory will come back to me, and I will have a little weep and move on. In either case, unfortunately, I end up a blotchy, snotty mess.

I swapped the horrendous anxiety I had been experiencing while Herbie was ill, for clinical depression. I have a history of depression so I knew what it was and why I was feeling it and I decided, in agreement with my GP, I would treat it naturally. I used diet, sleep and a personalised Bach flowers remedy. I am still a little depressed twelve months on, but I am functioning well and continue to work at it.

The deal is, if it gets very bad, I'll go back to my GP. At the moment, I'm coping.

Other people may need medical intervention. If you are so lost that you can't sleep or eat, or if you have difficulty engaging with other people or working, you really should seek medical help. Depression is a terrible illness and it needs to be treated. There are a range of options available to sufferers, so take some good advice.

Nobody would think badly of you for being depressed after the loss of your best friend. In life's great scheme, if you're going to be depressed about something, I think the deaths of those you love and who love you, must rate pretty highly!

Listen to those closest to you. Sometimes they can see what you cannot. If other people suggest you see the GP, think about it. Sometimes you get so lost in depression, you can't see the wood for the trees. You may not realise quite how badly you are suffering. Professional help now, may save you a long period of misery.

On the other hand, remember that depression is a completely normal reaction to the loss of your best friend. Why shouldn't you feel deeply sad?

Depression is an entirely normal, appropriate and valid response to loss. In fact, it would be more unusual to not feel depressed after a death. Depression is a step in the process of healing, and it will take the time it takes to disperse.

5. Acceptance

We don't all reach the final stage. If your pet's death was extremely sudden it can be hard to ever feel 'right' again. The thing to remember is that 'acceptance' of your best friend's loss does not mean you're suddenly happy and life is hunky dory again. It simply means you are out of depression, you know your pet is not coming back and the anger has gone.

We learn to live with what is our 'new normal'. Our landscape has changed and we have to adapt. Sometimes we hold on to parts of our old life – we keep toys and leads, baskets and mementoes. I have a box where I keep some veterinary bills (there were lots of those after all), and Herbie's collar and a rosette. Silly little things. I've kept his blanket too.

Other people get rid of everything. My Dad does this when he loses a pet. It is not a betrayal of his dogs. He misses his as much as I miss mine, but what works for him and what works for me, is different. In time you replace 'things' but you can never replace memories.

This whole five stage process of grieving can take years to complete, if indeed it is ever completed. I keep saying it, but grief is a deeply personal experience, and it is yours to own. You choose to let others share it or not, but at the end of the day, no-one can take your pain away. You need to feel the grief as it takes you.

Please remember, this five stage process will not be linear, it will not be smooth. I prefer to see it as three steps forward and two steps back. You may never get to the end, but as long as you have forward trajectory, things will get better.

8. SMALL THINGS YOU CAN DO THAT MAY HELP EASE YOUR GRIEF

Two thoughts that really helped me through my initial grief.

Resistance is futile

This silly saying, 'resistance is futile', is one of my favourites and has been something I've told myself for years ever since watching *Star Trek: The Next Generation*. When Herbie passed away, a friend of mine who had lost her dog two months before, wrote to me:

> *"I read a lovely piece about grief being like bobbing in the sea with the waves crashing over you. At first it's non-stop but gradually the waves lessen. Some days the waves get whipped up and return. Just like the sea there's no control, you just have to let them come and go."*

You just have to cling on and go with the ebb and flow of your feelings. That was an analogy that I held on to. This really resonated with me at the time and I would remind myself of it when I was beating myself up for feeling so lost and sad.

Step into your pain

Another friend of mine highlighted an article about living with the pain of grief. Essentially what it was saying is that bereavement tends to leave us with mixed feelings. We feel guilt, anger, hurt, heartbreak etc. and sometimes we wallow in our own misery. Some of us live in the past for a while, thinking about what was, and what we have lost. Others decide they need to move on, and they ignore their feelings of grief. Neither approach is particularly healthy.

One way to help yourself through the grieving process is to 'step into the circle of your pain'. Embrace it. Own your pain. When the wave crashes over you, don't dismiss it, instead feel it. I found myself telling myself things like, "Oh this hurts. I'm really missing him. I'm allowed to feel sad. I'm allowed to be devastated." In addition to this I would tell myself, "I'm OK. I am loved. He loved me. I loved him. I *love* him."

If we don't lock our grief away, but own it and live in it, we experience it fully and acknowledge that we're allowed to feel this way. That's empowering for us. It is hard to do, especially at the beginning when we want to hide from our feelings or we're in denial, but it helps us move forward.

Talk to yourself about your love for your best friend in the *present tense*. I **love** him or her. It keeps your best friend close. And it is true – you do love him or her, you haven't suddenly stopped loving them. Love is such an important and valid emotion so hold onto it.

It may sound daft, but it really does work. Stepping into your pain means acknowledging your own feelings of love and hurt. It means validating both your existence and the existence of your dog. As times goes on, when you use this method, there comes a point at which the pain will come over you, and you will nod at it, acknowledge it, and then you'll breathe, and the pain will pass again. It will come back soon enough, but that's ok. You know you can deal with it.

Sometimes I welcome the sharp pain I get when I stumble on Herbie's absence afresh, because for just a moment I had forgotten he was gone – and the sharp pain just means I'm connecting with my love for him and his for me once more. That's a nice thing.

Other things you can do to help yourself

You have placed a bookmark on your heart for your dog, and everything you do in the first few days will be in honour of him or her. You'll be trying to be a caretaker of their lives and your memories. That's all well and good, but you also have to look after yourself.

The first thought you need is, "**hold on**." Just keep holding on. Keep breathing.

Accept any **support** that is offered to you. People may offer you time off work, or to walk your other dogs, or cook dinner. Take it. They won't be offering in a few days. Grab yourself some 'you' time to do what you need to do. To sit, to cry, to walk alone. Whatever.

Get some rest. Even if you can't sleep, you should take time out, lie down and close your eyes. Rest is better than nothing. Nap if you can.

Make a cosy safe space for yourself, with blankets and pillows. Curl up. Drink green tea or something soothing. Be in the moment.

Forgive yourself for absent-mindedness. Make lists, or write things down. In the initial days after loss, we all forget things. It is very hard to concentrate and focus on what needs doing. You have time.

Cry. Cry for as long as you need, when you need. In public, in private, wherever. Dr Seuss said, "Be who you are, say what you feel, because those who mind don't matter, and those who matter don't mind." I think that's a great approach to your personal grief. If you need to cry but want to do it succinctly, watch a sad movie or read a sad book. My personal favourite is to cry in the shower.

Talk to people if they will let you. You can reach out to bereavement organisations if you have no-one else, or use online forums. I'm including some resources for these at the end of the book.

If talking is out of the question, **write it down**. I was so lost in my loneliness, but I did find that writing helped. I have some bits and bobs saved. Writing allows you to be brutally honest, and as soppy as you like. It can help you understand what you're feeling and why. You can share it if you like, or you can keep it private.

Make sure you take some **exercise**. It doesn't have to be strenuous, but keep moving as this will boost the serotonin levels in your body and lift your spirits. I have to be honest, being out and about and seeing nature without Herbie hurt me for months. Walking among trees and hearing the leaves whisper in the breeze reduced me to tears. But I started to imagine him there with me, and now I think of him racing free and happy in the fields and among the trees as I walk. I can see some fields from my desk, so I often like to think of him racing around those, looping in great circles, tail wagging, barking. Full of life and joy!

If you need **help**, ask someone for it. It might just be to do your shopping for you, or it might be to make a phone call. It doesn't matter. Small acts of kindness from others will help you remain grounded.

You probably won't feel like it but you will need to **eat**. It is important to keep your blood sugar levels up as this keeps your mood swings in check. Water is also important. Stay hydrated.

Occasionally you'll find yourself short of oxygen and feeling stifled. Take time to **breathe** deeply. Fill your lungs, stretch your back, throw your shoulders back. Breathing helps to relieve stress.

Pray or meditate. Bring yourself back to a calm centre. It doesn't matter if you cry afterwards, but if you can truly find moments to listen to your breathing, it will give you a break from the constant noise you're dealing with in your head, I promise. There are some great meditation videos on YouTube. Perhaps they can help you?

When **laughter** and happiness enter your life embrace them. I did laugh a few times the day Herbie died. It was forced, but what is life without laughter? Keep practicing, because eventually it will be real and there will be joy once more.

Practice **gratitude**. Think of your best friend and list all the reasons why you are grateful they were in your life. Think about the people who have been kind to you since your best friend passed. This is a way of counting your blessings, and effectively, what you are doing is reminding yourself that the world is not all bad.

Stick to your **routines** as far as possible. If you don't, the disruption in your life will last much longer.

Take it at your own pace. **Grief just 'is'**. It is your journey. There is no schedule, and no-one has the right to say, "Oh, I thought you'd be over it by now." You'll be over it when you're over it.

Protect your mood. By this I mean, if you are prone to anxiety and depression, or even if you are feeling emotionally vulnerable, take steps to keep yourself on an even keel. As mentioned above, diet and exercise are important, but you also need to make sure you give yourself chances to sleep and rest, and avoid stimulants as far as possible (alcohol, caffeine and nicotine for example). I'm my own worst enemy really, because in moments of high stress I feed my tendency for insomnia with large doses of coffee. It is not a good idea.

Write letters. You can do what I did and write a letter from your pet to yourself, or you can write to your pet. I did this with Toby. I wrote letters and poured my heart out and then I sealed them and hid them away in among my books. I found some of them when I was moving a few years ago. I destroyed them without re-reading them.

The advantage of such letters is that you can be as emotional as you like, and it is a safe and private space. You will preserve their memory in your mind. Don't worry that it is morbid to do this, there's nothing unusual about wanting to maintain the loving connection you had with your dog. Preserving Herbie's memory is something I do every day. It keeps him closer to me.

Rainbow Bridge

You've probably heard of Rainbow Bridge. It is a based on a poem from the 1980s (author unknown) that talks of a paradise where pets go when they die. They wait at the Bridge, and they are young and healthy and happy once more. They get to play and frolic with all of their furry friends. Then one day, they prick their ears up and go crazy with happiness, because finally you are walking towards them and you are reunited with your best friend. You get to cross the Rainbow Bridge together.

It's totally charming, and you know what? We don't know what happens when we pass away, so why can't it be true? If there is a heaven, I know my Herbie will be waiting for me.

What else brings comfort?

Lynda brought Buttons home because she wanted her children to say goodbye, then she took her to a private pet crematorium, collected her ashes the next day and personally chose her casket.

After the loss of Dirk, Sarah found spending time with her other three dogs and making a fuss of them helped a lot. She also, liked to look at photos and videos of Dirk before he was ill, and remember what a brilliant life he had and how spoiled he was. She had him cremated and scattered in his favourite places which she found therapeutic. She says that knowing he had the best possible life and that he knew he was loved helped her.

Helen looked at photos of Poppy too. "I looked at her pictures, I talked to friends, I talked to family, I looked back on pictures of her as a younger dog, right up to the day before she was put to sleep. I could then see, that she had changed drastically in weight etc. My pictures and videos of her helped me a lot, and after a few days, when talking to family, we talked about her funny antics, and laughed about them through our tears."

When Libby lost Barney, she went riding on her horse often, alone with thoughts of her boy, and like many found the support of friends and family a tremendous help. Helen said the same thing, and along with looking at pictures, and remembering wonderful memories, she says "admitting to myself that I did do everything I could," made her feel a little easier.

Heather says that initially the only way she coped was to put Diggs to the side of her mind. "I could not think about him, not about his beautiful little face and how he lost so much weight in the last few days." She was crying as she recalled it, when writing to me five months later. "I compartmentalised my grief. I felt and feel disloyal doing that but it was the only way I could survive."

✻✻✻

Things that definitely don't help

I decided to write this book because I had become acutely aware of the phrase, "he was just a dog." I realised that my grief transcended that tired notion, one that is tritely rolled out by people who think they're being helpful and supportive, but who invariably aren't and who just don't get it. Heather had this with Diggs, when people said to her, "he was just a dog." They would ask her, "How would you feel if it was a family member?" The thing is, most of us dog lovers, and certainly the people who will read this book, see our dogs as family members so this is a hurtful thing to be asked.

Lynda agrees that people are thoughtless, and the attitude of others, even family and close friends can be hurtful. "It's just a dog. You should be over it by now. People could not understand why I brought her home with me after she died. I had comments about the money I spent. The belief that getting another dog somehow is a replacement and you are OK now."

Libby notes there's a fine line to tread between support and intrusion on someone's grief. She didn't find it helpful when people constantly messaged her and sent photos of Barney. "For me it takes time for the open wounds to heal, I wasn't ready for that so soon."

Dog and pet bereavement do seem to bring out the insensitivity of many of our friends and colleagues. It seems that some people imagine they can respond any way they choose, without considering how the bereaved feels. Helen found herself getting upset – rightly so - when some acquaintances told her it was time for Poppy to go!

9. WHEN WILL YOU BE OVER IT?

Hey, it's been twelve months as I publish this, and I'm still not over it. I may never be. But I am better than I was. It takes a long time to get over total devastation, but every day I put one foot in front of the other and I carry on. Some days are great, and some days are not so great, but I know that my life is enriched because Herbie spent nearly ten years of it with me. I thank my lucky stars he came into my life.

It takes time. I asked others how long it seemed to take for them to feel normal - and I felt better when I heard the replies. Listen to their experiences and see if you can relate.

Heather told me that, "after feeling like I wanted to be buried with my boy (Diggs) for weeks, I learned this tactic of putting my darling boy aside in my mind. I also felt like I was crying for myself, not for him. He was at peace, I was the one suffering and I was dwelling on that which was selfish."

The early weeks are the hardest. When Libby told me about Barney he had only been gone for just over three months. Libby said, "I certainly don't feel normal or better. The pain is just not quite so sharp anymore and I can look at photos of him and feel so proud of him and how lucky I was that he was mine. Then the tears come... and don't stop for ages."

Can you get back to normal? This varies between

71

individuals. Heather feels she is getting there. She aches for Diggs sometimes, but she's grateful and feels privileged to have had him in her life. "I no longer dwell on my grief, and I can think of other things, so that feels better."

However, getting back to normal does take time. Liz says that when Sara went, "my memories of her growing up with the kiddies when they were young, all came to the fore, and they keep coming back no matter how much I try and push them aside. I am happy to move on - I am - but things have changed."

For Sarah, who sees herself as a strong and positive person, she says, that after four months (when she wrote to me), "I feel a lot better ... until someone triggers a sad memory."

For Lynda, the journey was a long one. She says it took her about 18 months to feel better, but 'normal' was not the same as before. "I will never be the same as I was before losing Buttons. I think loss and grief changes you forever. I don't believe I am better, it is more to do with life moves on and I have gone along with it, and accepted that I cannot change the past." Lynda lost Buttons eight years ago.

I think Helen puts it best. "Every dog I lose, a bit of me goes too. You learn to live with their loss, but never truly get over it. You may forget for a while, but in my case it comes back, and you have immense sadness."

10. WHAT NEEDS TO BE DONE IN THE AFTERMATH?

In the immediate aftermath you will be reeling of course, but there are a few things you will need to do. Notify your pet insurance company is the first, and disposing of the remains is the second. If your dog did not pass away while at your vet's, it is a good idea to inform the practice of your dog's passing too.

Notify your insurance company

From a completely objective point of view, pet insurance is darned expensive these days, so the sooner you stop paying it the better. A quick phone call, armed with your policy number, should suffice. In my experience it is a relatively painless phone call and the person on the other end of the phone has always been sympathetic. Of course if your pet has been receiving veterinary care, it is likely your vet will attend to notifying the insurers when he or she send the final bill through. There is usually a box on the insurance claim form that asks whether the pet has died and what the cause of death was, and your vet is best placed to sort this for you

Disposal of remains

If your dog dies suddenly you have the option of disposing of the remains yourself or taking them to the vet. Your vet can then arrange a cremation, just the same way as he or she would if your dog died under their care.

You have two options if you have decided to go it alone. You can bury your dog in the garden or you can contact a local pet crematorium and take them there yourself.

Burial

Think carefully if you intend to bury your dog in the garden. Is this your home, owned outright? Do you intend to live there forever? If you have to move, could you bear the thought that your dog would remain in the garden. I have seen a number of instances where people have had to dig up their pets when they move. Now this can be pretty unpleasant, and if you will view the remains, this is not an image you want to live with.

Also consider whether your property is big enough. I know someone who had a complaint from her neighbours when she decided to bury her dog in her tiny garden. In the end, we persuaded her to cremate her lovely girl and sprinkle the ashes.

In the UK it is legal to bury a pet in the back garden of your own personal dwelling as long as your pet does not come under the category of hazardous waste. Why he should, I have no idea! Possibly, there might be issues with the water table? As always, if in doubt contact your local authorities to check. They will normally be sympathetic.

If you don't own your property yourself, you will need permission from the owner. My advice would be not to bury your pet in the garden of your rented property, because your tenure is not secure forever. You never know what might happen and you risk heartbreak if you have to move. Believe me, I've seen this come up on a number of forums a few times over the past twelve months. It's a very real problem.

If you choose to bury your best friend in the garden, the advice is to wrap them up well, in a blanket or sheet, and then wrap them with a strong plastic bag or sheet and seal tightly, and dig a deep hole. You don't want other pets, or foxes etc., getting the scent and coming along to dig your dog back up. That would be very distressing. Dig your hole at least four feet deep. You can use lime around the body as this will put other animals off. You may choose to place some small belongings in the grave with your dog.

Once that's done, pack the earth tightly above your pet, and remember that the ground will settle so you need to pack it tight. The beauty of burying your pet is you can mark the spot with a memorial of some sort, and you've always got somewhere to come back to.

Cremation

You may be given a choice of urn or casket by your vet or pet crematorium. If you like them, all well and good. If you don't like them, opt for the cheapest one and then search online for something you really love. My Mum and Dad found a beautiful one for their Yorkshire Terrier, Poppy.

If you opt for the pet crematorium and don't go through your vet, you may find that some crematoriums offer funeral services. You will need to enquire and there will be costs involved. You can search for more details online.

Hold a memorial service

See the next section for memorial service ideas. You may not have considered a memorial service. You don't hear of many people doing this, but why not? It's a wonderful way to honour and remember your best friend. You can celebrate his or her life by saying a few words, or by planting a tree or decorative bush, or go the whole hog and invite friends and family.

11. CEREMONIES

Planning a ceremony for your dog

I wrote in a blog at the time of Herbie's passing, that it is a shame there are no recognizable words for someone who loses a pet. You are not widowed or orphaned. However, there is no equivalent word in English for someone who loses a child either, so the feeling of being a 'parent' or a 'carer' or a 'responsible adult' who has experienced a bereavement is difficult to label.

In my case, I was 'Mum'. Even the vet addressed me as 'Mum'. Herbie understood the word 'Mum' in a way that he didn't know who 'Jeannie' was. I do understand though, that many pet owners don't anthropomorphosize their pets in the same way some of us do even though they love their dogs just as deeply. By the same token, some people need memorial services or ceremonies (not necessarily 'parents') and some people don't (not necessarily 'non-parent's), but this is an entirely individual decision.

I'm afraid this chapter will be a little stark, but let's just grit our teeth and talk about the practicalities we need to think about when our best friend has gone.

To have a ceremony or not?

If your pet is being buried at home, either the body, or an internment of the ashes when s/he comes back from a crematorium, it is only natural that if you want one, you can have a small ceremony at that stage.

You may be unable to bury your pet on your own

property, and elect to send your dog to a pet crematorium instead. You may think, 'well that's that'! However, I doubt the people who buy and read this book will be happy with just letting their dog go without so much as by-your-leave. With Toby (my dog before Herbie), I sent him to the pet crematorium via my vet and his ashes were returned in a casket with a certificate that told me the date and time of the cremation. That's lovely. I feel he was cared for, and that the crematorium thought about my feelings. I never considered having a ceremony for Toby because I hadn't believed it to be an option, and at the time, I felt quite alone in my grief.

In fact, before Herbie I never had a ceremony for a pet. I was not brought up in a faith and for many years considered myself an atheist, but I may have bowed my head and made a silent prayer to anyone or thing that was listening. I have lighted candles for my pets, grandparents and friends, both at home and in Christian churches, but I have never held a service, an order of things to do. The difference this time for me, and for Herbie, was that I have embraced a more spiritual side of myself over the past few years, something deeply personal with no single God, and I wanted to send Herbie home to the place I imagine in my head and my heart.

I can't tell you how much solace my little service gave me. It was an acknowledgement of Herbie's passing and of his worth to me. I was able to articulate my love, my pain, my guilt and my grief. I did it out loud. I cried - but that's okay.

The thing is, you love your best friend as though he or she

is one of the family. You wouldn't dream of not having a funeral for a member of your family, so what is the difference? You have every right to honour and celebrate your dog, so don't be ashamed or think people will consider you ridiculous. Who cares what they think at the end of the day? This is about you and your dog. By all means invite anyone else you know who will participate with love and good humour, but if they're going to scoff at you, don't bother.

Your ceremony

I would recommend taking some time to plan your ceremony and not do it off the cuff. You may need candles, mementos, photos, poetry, prayers or songs, so gather all those things together. Remember the aim of your ceremony is to honour and remember your friend, and speak your heart. You may ask everyone who is present to say a few words, or wax as lyrical as they wish. You will need to forewarn everyone what your plans are for the ceremony otherwise they may poo-poo what you're trying to do and this will be tremendously hurtful for you at a time when you're hoping to be serious and sincere. You won't get closure from this ceremony, I'm not going to lie, but you do draw a line on part of your grief, by acknowledging your friend has passed, and as we've seen, moving from the denial stage of grief is an important part of recovery.

Remember – if you want paw prints or hair clippings you should make sure you are prepared to this in advance or as part of the ceremony.

Consider where you are holding the ceremony. This could be in your garden, at a pet cemetery, at the place where you sprinkle the ashes or in your own home. You may have your pet there with you – whether his or her body or their ashes – or they may have already been taken care of.

Ceremony ideas

Light a candle for your pet. Then adapt one of the following blessings for your own personal use:

"During this time of grief, we light a candle in memory of _____. May the flame remind us of the warmth and love we feel for our special companion. May the light help guide our beloved pet to a place of peace and love. May the power of the flame give us strength on our healing journey as the sadness is gradually replaced by warm memories."

"We are gathered today to acknowledge the death of _____ who was _____'s special companion for (many) years and to honour the unique role that animals play in our lives. Not everyone understands the extent that a loss of a pet can affect us, and sometimes we can be surprised ourselves. Gathering for a memorial ceremony during this loss helps us to acknowledge its significance and to bring to light that the healing may take time as with any loss."

"Although we are saddened by the loss of (name) this is also an occasion to remember and celebrate his/her life and the special role that animals play in our lives. You are invited to share a memory of _____ or perhaps your own pet. It might be a special way you played, a particular nickname, or something that you learned from your dear companion."

"In addition to honouring _____'s life, we are here to acknowledge his/her passing from this earth. Death is a part of life's cycle even though it is hard to it understand intellectually or emotionally. We ask the Spirit of Life to be with us and usher _____ into the spirit world so that she can rest in peace."

Closing: There is a right time for everything. A time to laugh, a time to cry. A time to be born a time to die (Ecclesiastes)

Buddhist homage

Life and Death are but an illusion.

Happy and Sad are just a state of mind.

Love and Compassion alleviates the suffering

Of All sentient Beings — those who have been

our Mothers and our Fathers.

To recognize the interconnectedness of all beings

Is to know peace!

I found these Buddhist approaches to pet death on a website called *The Elephant Journal*. It was gathered together by N., a Shambhala Buddhist. He asked for advice after the death of his cat, and found most Buddhists felt it was appropriate to do a Sukhavati (a traditional Buddhist funeral in which one lets go of one's attachment to your loved one and wishes them well) ceremony, along with Tonglen, other kinds of bodhisattva (or compassion) practice and Mantras (chants), aspiration prayers and dedications.

One recommended short Tibetan chant suggested was:

> *"Oh Buddhas & Bodhisattvas of the ten directions and the three times,*
>
> *Please protect and guide (your animal's name) on her journey.*
>
> *May she be free from fear and clinging to this life.*
>
> *May she have a favourite rebirth."*

N, also received this mantra: NAMO SUGATA RATNA SHIKHIN which someone has used for dead and dying animals for many years and found it helpful to keep thoughts and feelings positive at difficult moments.

Farewell ritual

I modified this ritual for use with Herbie. It's by Patti Wigington and it's a Wiccan ritual, but again you can adapt it to your own faith or no faith. I knew Herbie was fading and so I had looked this up in advance and I had gathered the items I needed. I performed this, with my husband after the moon had come up on the day of his passing.

You will need:

- Salt
- A pink candle (pink to represent your love for your pet)
- Incense of your choice

- Water
- A stone to represent your pet
- A stone to represent yourself
- Four matching crystals that that have a meaning for you or your pet
- A small tray, plate or dish

The idea is that you arrange the salt, incense, candle and water in a circle to represent the four elements, and add one of your four matching crystals to each. Light the incense and the candle. Place the stones representing you and your pet in the dish in the centre.

Take a moment to meditate or reflect quietly. Focus on the two stones in the centre. One is you, and one is your pet. They should be side by side, touching each other, as you and your pet touched each other in life. Take both stones in your hands, and hold them tightly. As you do so, remember the positive and happy memories of your time with your pet.

Pass the stones over the salt, and say: <Pet's name>, with the energies of Earth, I am with you in spirit. Your memory will always remain with me.

Pass the stones over the incense, and say: <Pet's name>, with the energies of Air, I am with you in spirit. Your memory will always remain with me.

Pass the stones over the candle, and say: <Pet's name>, with the energies of Fire, I am with you in spirit. Your memory will always remain with me.

Pass the stones over the water, and say: <Pet's name>, with the energies of Water, I am with you in spirit. Your memory will always remain with me.

You should then place the two stones back in the dish in the centre of the circle. Collect up the four matching crystals or gemstones and add them to the dish as well.

Now tell your dog (or other pet) how much you will miss them, and how grateful you are that you and he shared a journey together. If other people are with you, they should also place a matching stone in the dish and talk to your dog about what they will miss about their presence.

If your dog left you in traumatic circumstances talk about that too. Tell them how happy you are that they are free of pain and fear. If you had your dog put to sleep, tell them why you did this. Tell them how hard it was for you. Speak from your heart. If you feel guilt, talk about it, but tell him or her it would have been incredibly selfish for you to delay your own pain at the expense of their pain.

Close your eyes and reflect on the life you and your dog had together, and remember how different it would have been without them. Think of the love you had, that you still have. If you need to cry or scream or shout, now is the time to do it. This ceremony should touch the open flame of your pain.

Finally, take the dish with all the stones in it, and pass it to everyone involved in the ritual. Allow each person to hold it for a moment. Hold your hand lightly above the stones and feel the energy emanating from them.

Conclude the ritual in whatever way you wish. In my case I whispered goodbye and blew the candle out and watched as the smoke curled and dissipated.

What I loved about this ceremony was that the stones in the dish are then placed in your dog's favourite place – the place you would expect to see them – and left for a few days. I placed my stones in Herbie's basket under my desk. Then every time you look at the place, still half expecting your dog to be there, you say 'hello', and 'I love you' and you let them know you are remembering them. That gave me comfort.

When you're ready you can put the stones in a safe place, perhaps a little bag, or in a special box. Or you can make the stones into a necklace or add them to a memorial somewhere. You can give a stone to everyone that wants to remember your dog.

In my case, Herbie's stones are in his memory chest with my other keepsakes. Occasionally when I'm missing him badly, I'll hold a stone until it's warm and remember him.

What's important about your ceremony??

You don't have to have a religious ceremony of any kind. You need to choose something that works for you and the memory you have of your best friend. At the very least, a few heartfelt words and memories spoken out loud will be special. At this time of deep pain, ask yourself what you want. Your dog would be happy if you were happy, and they wouldn't have understood the concept of a ceremony or a ritual or even an afterlife, so this is purely for you. That's as valid a reason as you need. Make it beautiful. You and your best friend deserve that.

Also, if you feel silly, or you think your feelings would be invalidated by friends or family due to their lack of understanding, do it alone. Take yourself off for a walk or go into the garden and vocalise your own thoughts where no-one can hear you.

One thing your dog would understand would be the love you send after them, and I know you'll be emanating that in bucket loads. Good for you. The world needs more people who love dogs.

12. CONSIDERING YOUR OTHER PETS

How to help your other pets cope

I've read a number of articles that discuss whether the remaining dogs in your pack actually grieve for their lost friend, with some writers suggesting they don't. That's not my experience, and while it seems sensible that at the very least your remaining dog or dogs will pick up on your stress and sadness, I think dogs do grieve in their own way even if they don't understand the concept of loss or death.

It isn't just you who has lost a friend. If you have more than one dog, part of the pack has disappeared. I was acutely aware when I clipped Herbie's lead on to his collar on that final morning, that I probably wouldn't be bringing him home to our other two dogs, Satin and Betsy. I think my husband was in denial, but I definitely wasn't. I didn't know how to say to the dogs, 'Maybe this is goodbye' but I know I paused and let them sniff and fuss him and then I settled them down and I took Herbie away.

When I returned the house was so quiet. I had his collar and lead and Satin and Betsy sniffed it. Of course they were bound to pick up on my mood, and I was beside myself with grief, so it was a horrible subdued day punctuated by me sobbing and weeping as I needed to, and Betsy nudging me occasionally, worried about me, I guess.

The question is, how much did the other two dogs understand? I don't know is the answer. I think they knew he was ill. They had been increasingly gentle around him. And now here I was returning home without him. Satin especially was lost. She was older than Herbie by four years, so she was his 'Mum' when he first came home as a puppy.

Betsy was a strange case. I never felt that she and Herbie got on as well as Betsy and Satin, and Herbie and Satin, but actually it was Betsy who seemed to become very dejected and quiet. She stopped playing, she stopped wagging her tail. When my husband and I came home with her after we had all been out, she would rush into our bedroom and look on top of the bed, Herbie's habitual resting place. I know she was looking for him. Even when we moved she did the same thing. Herbie had never been inside the new house, but for a long time she would run into the house, dash up the stairs and inspect the top of the bed. I really felt for her. I was mentally doing exactly the same thing.

I read somewhere a few years ago that you should let your pets share the loss when the time comes. There was some research that looked at allowing pets to be there at the time of euthanasia. I had considered this in the weeks up to letting Herbie go, because it seemed sensible, but on the morning I left for the vet, I couldn't really have coped with anything else. It took everything I had not to throw myself on the floor and scream. Instead I very carefully put one foot in front of the other, reassured my husband, and stowed Herbie in the car. And all the time, I KNEW.

Your pets have spent so much time together – sharing the same beds and sofas, playing together, walking together, eating together, squished up in the boot of the car or their crate together. They have bonded, they love and trust each other, they recognise the sound of each other's collars and leads.

Grief therefore shows itself in a number of different ways. With Betsy, it was her complete loss of joy, but with your dog it might be a loss of appetite, toileting accidents in the house, barking, or a change of temperament. As long as you know there isn't a medical reason (such as an illness or an injury) for this behaviour, you can deal with it as you deal with your own grief, with lots of love and reassurance.

I'm not sure I was very good at that initially, because the boy I wanted wasn't there, but actually I came to see quite quickly that I wanted to protect my remaining 'family': my girls. For the remainder of summer 2016, the girls were pretty much with my husband and I everywhere we went, and as we were moving house, and running our gift shop this was complicated at times. In the end, I think we were able to console each other, but it took time, for Betsy especially, to relax and become more like her old self.

In a period of upset it is important to maintain routines for your other pets as far as possible. Try to feed and walk them at the usual times. I'm sad to say that to this day I have not gone back on the walk that I used to love to take Herbie on, but I plan to do that on his first anniversary. The day I publish this book. I'll take flowers and I am going to tie a blue ribbon to our special tree.

The Ralph Site advise minimising any sources of distress or stress to your other pets if they appear to be grieving, so don't leave them alone for extended periods or leave them in kennels at this troubled point in your family lives.

Should I let my remaining pets see the deceased one?

This question is obviously more or less applicable depending on where euthanasia will be performed. Research suggests dogs and probably cats and other friends like rabbits and guinea pigs do benefit from being able to see and smell the body of the deceased pet. Experts think that by recognising the other animal to be dead it provides an explanation for the surviving companion about their sudden disappearance. Allowing surviving pets to see the deceased one can help to minimise how long the grief lasts and how deep it is, and even if it doesn't, it is unlikely to worsen the situation.

If you are in a position to have your friend put to sleep among their own surroundings at home, then of course any other pets may be present unless you choose to shut them away, perhaps because they are not friendly or they become too boisterous around visitors. Some vets recommend that other pets see the body of the deceased pet before he or she is taken away to prevent aimless wandering around and searching in the days afterwards.

I would suggest going with your gut instinct about this. For me, I knew I was moving within a few weeks and I didn't want to tie Herbie emotionally to my old house. It had only been a temporary home, one I didn't love, and I wouldn't be coming back, so I didn't want to feel that Herbie was 'there'. There was no question therefore that his passing would take place at the surgery. I'd have loved for him to have lived in our new house, but I'm glad I spared him the disruption of moving at a time when he was incredibly poorly.

One thing to be careful about is that if you are burying your departed friend's body in the garden, it is probably best not to let a dog see where - as this may lead to him/her trying to dig the body up.

Symptoms your dog might exhibit after a loss

It's important to remember that every dog is an individual. If you own more than one dog, you'll be quite well aware of this. Every dog will react differently. Pay attention to each of them and try and support them.

Common dog reactions to loss of a pack member

- Loss of appetite
- Drinking less water
- Lethargy
- Illness
- Personality change
- No playfulness
- Howling or barking
- Showing signs of aggression
- No reaction at all. "Where's my dinner, Mum and Dad?"

What you should do for your remaining dog/s

Stick as closely as possible to your normal routine. Your dog needs to feel everything is just as it was, so walk them and feed them and play with them just the way you normally would. If there are physical symptoms keep a close eye out. It may not be that your dog is mourning at all, they may be ill themselves.

Remember the dog that was lost was their companion and playmate, so who will take that role on now? You may need to offer more stimulation and activity than you normally would, otherwise the remaining dog or dogs could become bored, destructive or anxious. What can you do to make up for this loss of stimulation? Well, take your dog for an extra walk, play fetch in the garden or park, play with tuggy toys or join an obedience class, or perhaps start an activity with them such as Flyball.

It would be unusual for a dog to mourn for a long period, although I'm sure we've all seen posts on the internet that show a dog visiting the grave of their owner every day for years. Animals in the wild have to move on extremely quickly, and you will want your remaining dogs to do that, even if you're struggling yourself.

13. THE NEXT STAGE OF GRIEVING

After the practicalities have been taken care of, and after the first fire of grief has subsided a small amount, you enter another phase. At this stage you'll have a strange mixture of numbness and pain probably. I know I did. I had accepted that Herbie had gone, and that I had made the right decision, but the finality of it was total. I walked around for weeks feeling as though someone had filled my insides with stone.

On one level I coped. I walked and talked and worked and functioned like a proper adult. I had conversations with people. I cooked dinners. I ate some, I slept some. But every time I closed my eyes, I would cry. And I would sit in front of the television and not see what was on. I felt cocooned in misery really. Every cell and fibre of my being cried out for my lad and I couldn't have him back.

I kept quiet about it on the whole. I didn't think anyone wanted to hear how desperately sad and unhappy I was, how lonely. I tried to talk about it with my husband, but he was moving on, whereas I wasn't. I was incredibly isolated in my grief. I wrote a few bits and pieces and put them on Facebook and was grateful for the friends who supported me, but again I was scared to overdo it in case people started thinking, "Oh Jeannie please. He was just a dog."

Well he wasn't just a dog to me. He was my soul dog. My best friend. The child I never had.

I looked for him everywhere. I felt closest to him in the

study because that's where we had spent so much time together when I was writing, and I had left his basket in its place next to my desk. The stones I used in his ritual were also there in the dish, and it felt very peaceful to me. Unfortunately, as I've mentioned, we were due to move house four weeks after he passed, so I had to pack everything up. I left his basket as long as I could, and it was a huge wrench for me to disturb it eventually.

When we moved into our new house, I placed his basket next to my desk again, and it is still here. Very worn. Betsy likes to use it, so there is some continuity there. I guess someday I'll part with it, but not yet.

By moving, I felt that my connection to Herbie was broken and I went through a really bad patch where I was lost and angry. I wanted to feel Herbie near me, and in the new house that didn't seem possible because Herbie had never been inside it, had never watered (wee-d on) the plants in the garden or explored the kitchen looking for scraps.

And then something miraculous happened. I opened a Groupon email, something I rarely do, and there was an offer for naming a star, and I didn't think twice. I paid my money and named a star - Herbie Longfellow Alderdice in my best boy's honour. He's up there in Ursa Major in the Northern hemisphere all year round. We had excellent clear skies in September and October 2016 and I would stand outside in my new garden and stare up at the heavens after dark, and wonder which of the stars winking down at me was my boy. It makes me feel so much better knowing that no matter where I am in the Northern

Hemisphere I can look up and think of him. I feel a lot of love for him, and for his star when I gaze at the skies. It's our love, because now that he is gone, we are one.

I'm not alone in this. Liz writes of Sara, "when she died I still took her lead some mornings and walked to our special place where there are a collection of oak trees and years ago I sat in front of them, expecting Sara to run off as I sat still, but she stood beside me and waited with me."

Strange occurrences

Some people will tell you that they experience unusual occurrences after their dog has passed away. The same things happen after other animals and humans have died and are apparently perfectly normal during the grief process and nothing to worry about. If they happen to you – take comfort in them. I felt the presence of my childhood friend Ted, a golden retriever, after he passed away while I was at University. It felt like he'd come to say goodbye and was wagging his tail very hard. Perhaps it was just a draught, who knows? I cherished that moment and always have.

Things you may experience in the aftermath of the passing of your friend

You may think you can smell, see, hear, or feel them.

You may remember them while wearing rose tinted spectacles. In my house, once my sense of humour had returned, we started to call Herbie, St. Herbie, because I couldn't remember him doing anything naughty. I still can't, really! But apparently you do begin to have more realistic memories as time goes by. Pfft! Herbie never did anything wrong!

You may not be able to remember what they looked or sounded like at all. This is just your grieving mind playing tricks on you. It will all come back.

You may be afraid that you will forget them. Trust me, you won't.

You may carry small things that remind you of your dog. Do what feels right for you.

You may feel that you are obsessing or dangerously preoccupied with thoughts of your dog. You have every right to be, you're grieving. However, try and keep one foot in the real world too.

You may have vivid dreams of your dog. This is one of my favourite things. Occasionally I do, and I'll hear his distinctive bark when I'm half asleep, and it is so comforting. It can be disturbing but it is normal.

***

To give you an example of where I was a few months after Herbie's death I've included a note I wrote. We had moved into our new home, Finley (my new puppy) was growing fast, and the trees had started to change colour and shed their leaves. I had a terrible fear of letting the summer go. The summer of 2016 belonged to Herbie and I wanted it always to be summer, so that he would always remain with me.

Here's what I wrote.

Herbie …

I've realised with a jolt that it's been 10 weeks today since I lost you. I don't count the days so much anymore but I'm always aware that Friday is the anniversary, and then I think of 'that' Friday and of course I weep. Weeping is not a good idea when I'm in the shop. Sometimes people ask me if I have a cold. I let them believe that's what it is. Grief is a virus I can't shake off.

When I say I'm not counting the days, that doesn't mean I'm not aware of the lack of you every single moment of time. Perhaps the only time I'm not hurting is when I'm asleep, but actually, who knows what I'm dreaming of? I don't remember my dreams the way I used to when I was younger. All I know is that every time I wake up, I realise with a jolt that you're not here anymore, and that you haven't simply left the room. I'll never stroke you again, never hug you, never kiss the top of your soft head, never feel the silkiness of your fur. This seems like an impossibility, but I guess this is why bereavement hurts so much.

I had to pause there for a moment and collect myself. I was lost in a sad reverie, remembering that last morning. Remembering your paw. Now the knot is in my throat and my eyes are burning. I can't swallow and I can't breathe. Was this journal such a good idea? It brings back memories, makes me think about things and that's painful.

I'm in the shop alone. No customers. No-one to reach out to, to say, "I'm hurting, I'm lonely, I miss my boy," please comfort me. Please commiserate with me. It's a tide of emotion and it is hard to hold it in check. I need a tissue and a cup of tea. That gives me an excuse to go out the back and pull myself together.

Your Dad said I should use the journal to catalogue the good times, to help me get past the block I'm feeling, so I should do that. This morning we were talking about how I am seeing so much of Finley growing up – and yet I find it hard to remember you as a puppy. We worked out that for the first five years or so, I was leaving home at 7.20 am to get into work. That was early. How did we spend any time together?

I know we did and I know I wanted to be at home with you. You were what I longed for throughout the day. To come home to your ecstatic welcome – it made that awful long commute all worthwhile.

I remember the horrible conversation with my boss when redundancy happened, and even though I said "I'll think about it," to him, my heart had already said, "Go home, stay home. Be with your boy. Find a way to be with your boy." That was by far the best outcome of losing my job.

And then you became my writing companion. You lay under the desk. You started off with the floor, and then I put a blanket down and eventually I had to buy you a second basket.

You were always a one for your comforts. Not for you a hard floor or the concrete. In fact, you weren't that keen on the ground at all. At the very least I had to lay a blanket down, and usually a cushion as well. You loved the purple sofas we had until we moved to Devon. I had to bring the end cushions with me even after we'd sent the rest of the furniture to the tip, because I knew you'd miss that sofa so much. I still have those stupid cushions. I'll keep them forever probably.

And the sneaky way you had of getting up on the bed. You were always allowed on the bed when I was reading, and then you knew the rule. I'd say, "Right Herbs, time to sleep. In your basket," and you'd gracefully jump down to the floor and into your basket next to me. I could reach out and stroke you whenever I wanted to.

Then you'd wait until your Dad and I had fallen asleep and up you'd get. Graceful and as light as a feather, right? You never disturbed us. We'd wake up and you'd have inculcated yourself into the gap between us and then… ever so slowly …. stretched … out. Such a clever boy.

And so I suppose that's why I'm so aware that you're not with me when I wake up in the night.

But those are the sort of memories to hold onto, right?

Love you darling,

Mum xxx

That was written in the middle of October and you can see how preoccupied I was with my memories of him, and how lost I felt.

I'd love to wave a magic wand and say you will feel better in X number of days if you do this and that. Unfortunately, what became increasingly clear to me as I researched and wrote this book, is that grief is a journey we take alone. Some people feel better in a few weeks or months and others take much longer. As I was completing this chapter I turned over my calendar because it was July 1st. Suddenly, eleven months on, I was weeping again, because July was Herbie's month and he never saw the end of it.

I had been beating myself up about my grief, but now I see

that it is perfectly normal and acceptable to grieve deeply for a long period of time. Lynda lost Buttons in December 2008, but she told me that "I still feel low. I'm typing all this with the tears flowing. Her birthday and the anniversary of her death makes me feel really low. As the years have gone by, it seems more apparent how close those dates are. Sometimes grief just comes to me for no reason, and other times it is when I read of others losses because I know how awful it is. 8 ½ years. It is a long time and sometimes it seems a lifetime ago, and sometimes only yesterday."

For Sarah too, hearing about other losses brings it all back. "I am on various forums about deerhounds, I just try to offer sympathy or advice, but it is still upsetting to hear about other dogs and their owners going through the same thing."

Liz misses her evening cuddles with Sara on the sofa, but Helen has no set pattern of grief. "It can happen when I'm shopping in a supermarket."

Heather experiences loss in numerous ways, rather like I do with Herbie. She says, "there are times when I feel low. When I stand and look at his photo; when I pass the veterinary surgery and I think of how he breathed his last in there; when I find one of his toys that I hadn't noticed before. I sometimes lay in bed and start to think of those horrible last days and my heart aches. Did I do my best? I have to pull my thoughts away."

Don't we all share these thoughts and feelings? Couldn't we all write that ourselves?

14. HELPING YOUR CHILDREN COPE

If you have children in the home, you'll know how close they can become to our pets. When your dog dies, you need to handle the situation sensitively and honestly in a way that is appropriate for their age, and your religion or beliefs. Try not to frighten them, or let them think that death is something they should fear. You also want to make sure they don't feel guilty for any reason, which may be hard for you if you're experiencing feelings of guilt yourself.

Breaking the news

This is probably the hardest part. Break the news somewhere your child feels safe, and you're unlikely to be disturbed. You want to allow them to express their emotions, whether that's through crying or being angry, so it's important they feel able to do that and are able to take the time they need.

From there you'll need to figure out how much information they should have. If they are pressing you for details, you'll need to make that call yourself, depending on how mature you think they are, and how they are likely to process any information you give them.

If your dog was old or had been poorly, ideally you will have spoken about losing him or her in the past, and have paved the way for sad news, but obviously, if your dog died suddenly, you won't.

Things to consider saying to your child, include:

- The Vet (or doggie doctor) did everything possible
- Our dog would never have become well again
- We did the kind thing and let her fall asleep
- It was really peaceful and loving
- Our dog wasn't scared
- We're so proud of our dog
- We'll always love her

You'll then have to answer the questions, and depending on your child's age you can talk about what death is, and how the vet sends a dog to sleep.

In the event that your child knows in advance that your dog will be passing away, you need to decide whether your child should be there with you and the vet or not. It can be quite traumatic for adults, so think carefully about whether experiencing this will comfort your child.

Choose your language carefully

Many children, especially autistic children, take words very literally. If you say your dog was 'put to sleep' this could be misconstrued as something temporary. Or they may start to imagine that sleeping can somehow kill you. If your child then has to have anaesthesia at a later stage, they will worry about the consequences of being put under.

When your dog's death is sudden

Be as calm as you can be and explain what happened to your dog if their death was sudden. Spare the details, but provide as much information as you feel able to.

Afterwards

Always let your child express their feelings for as long as they need. They may want a ceremony, or they may want to pray. Even if that's not your wish, accommodate your child where you can. You can discuss the afterlife, or reincarnation, or heaven.

Be honest

Don't lie and say your dog ran away, or has gone on holiday. Your child will feel the loss anyway, but this will be mixed with hope that the dog will come back. We know our best friend is not coming home, don't we? Let's not make things worse.

If you don't know the answers to any questions your child asks you, just tell them you don't. Do any of us really understand the mysteries of life and death?

Your child's emotions

Just like you, your child is going to be juggling a full range of emotions. They'll experience sadness, loneliness, anger, frustration and guilt. Let them talk about it whenever they wish, and encouraged them to draw or paint or write things down if that will help. Keep them active too.

You don't have to display a stiff upper lip yourself, either. If your children see that you're sad about your best friend, they'll realise that grief is natural and normal, and not a dirty secret that needs to be kept hidden. Don't scare them with the depth of your pain, but yes, cry with them if it helps. Share lots of stories and laugh at the funny things your dog did. It will be great therapy for you too.

Help them move on.

Moving On

If you are planning a ceremony and a memorial, let your child get involved. They can play a role, or they can write down a little speech or make a card. Perhaps they would like to make a scrapbook. These days we don't have as many physical copies of photographs, but you can download some and print them out, or you can create virtual photo albums. If in doubt, Google is your friend.

Emphasise that the pain does go away eventually. You may not believe that yourself, but it's a good thing to say.

15. HELPING YOUR OLDER RELATIVES

Sometimes when an older person loses a pet, it is even more of a desperate situation. I know this because my Dad lost his young Cairn, Lewis, in 2015, and he was inconsolable. He has moved on, but nothing takes that pain away. It broke my heart, because I was able to do nothing for him.

Do watch out for your parents and older friends. Losing a beloved dog later in life can lead to increasing isolation, and can trigger depression. I hate that my parents won't consider getting another dog because they think 'they're too old'. The loss of a dog throws up our own mortality. I'd recommend considering rescuing older dogs who may only have a few years left. It's a noble thing to do, and the mutual companionship will be wonderfully beneficial to both parties.

If you have concerns about your elderly relatives walking or looking after a pet because of health issues, consider getting in touch with The Cinnamon Trust.

The Cinnamon Trust in a voluntary organization that seeks to preserve the relationship between owners and their pets. It has a national network of over 15,000 community service volunteers who help in all manner of ways including walking the dog for a housebound owner, fostering if an owner is in hospital, and they supply emergency cards so that if an owner is taken ill away from home, the emergency services or hospital, know there is a pet at home.

16. MEMORIALS

From the moment I knew I was going to lose Herbie, I wanted him to be present with me in every moment. I feared his loss, and I was scared I would forget what he smelt like, what he looked like, what he sounded like, how he felt, so I set about organising a treasure chest and keeping things.

I looked everywhere for a chest that was big enough, eventually finding one on the Internet. I had thought I would decorate it but I haven't done that yet. It is so 'Herbie' to just be plain and clean and calm and still. Anything busier would not do.

In Herbie's chest I have his ashes, some photos and rosettes, his collar, his vaccination records and the candle and stones that I used for his farewell ceremony. I also have a few vet bills and the tooth that I found in his basket in November 2015, along with a few really weird things like a square of canvas cut from my whirly washing line that reminds me of the time spent in the garden with him. Somewhere in my loft I have a few puppy toys and one day I'll put those in the chest too.

My vet shaved off some of the fur from his head and put it in an envelope for me, so I still have that. I regret that I don't have his paw print.

To be honest, I don't look in the chest very often, I just have it near me, so that I know he's there. It's a comfort. I do however have the most beautiful portrait painted while he was still alive that is on the wall to the left of the desk where I write. I love to glance over and see him there.

Sometimes, when I'm feeling down because he's not with me, or I am reminded of him for some reason and tears come to my eyes, it is enough just to look at his beautiful face in that picture and remind myself of the love we shared and how grateful I am that we had our time together.

The other thing I have is a cushion with a photo of his face on. I found a company who can put any photo on a cushion, and I just loved the idea. I know a few people have said they couldn't do that for whatever reason, but I can't tell you the comfort it brings me at night when the tears come all too easily. I just touch it and I feel him close. It's also portable, so when I went away for the first time after Herbie had passed away, I took the cushion with me and it helped me feel that I wasn't 'leaving him behind'.

That's me, but there are so many ideas you can try if you're looking to memorialise your pet. Here's just some of them.

Urn or chest

Choosing the right resting place for your dog may or may not be important. For me, it really didn't matter because as far as I'm concerned, that's not really Herbie. Having said that, I cried buckets when I received his ashes back in his little wooden chest, and the inscribed plaque has been stroked a million times.

You may have a decent choice of urns and chests depending on your vet or who is providing the cremation service (if that is what you've chosen). You'll find that they come in lots of shapes and sizes and materials. Some offer personalization, and with others you just have an engraved plaque. With my old dog Toby, I was really disappointed to find the casket had been screwed shut. It's not that I wanted to inspect the ashes (some people do and that's okay) but just that I wanted to have the option of scattering his ashes at a time and place of my choosing. Now I am going to have to break into his box.

Headstone or memorial stone

You may want a headstone or a memorial stone. A search on the Internet will help you find a variety of companies who will provide these for you in a variety of materials and of variable quality. You can get stones in granite, marble or stone, and there are various novelty or fun and humorous options too. As with all of these decisions, you may wish to wait awhile and see what you decide upon once the initial pain and panic have passed.

Create a photo album or a montage

I still struggle to look at photos without crying, but other people are able do this quite soon after their loss and find solace in it. You can either print all your photos out and put them in an album to flick through as and when you need to, or create a collage and frame it. There are some services online that allow you to upload your photos and create a print book or album and this looks really special. You may be offered the chance to create a custom cover, or add text too.

Videos

You can create a moving montage of your pet using photos that you have stored online and add a voiceover or music. There are apps that can help you with this, or you can hire a professional to do it for you.

Have a picture painted

I do recommend this! Find a decent artist by browsing through their online galleries. Make sure you like the style they use before you commission them. Check out various Facebook dog pages and ask for recommendations, or google online. You need to be prepared to pay for the privilege of something wonderful, but you'll treasure it forever.

I have one of Herbie, painted while he was still alive, that I adore. A good friend of Helen's painted a picture of Poppy for her. Sarah would like one of Dirk just as soon as she can afford it.

Have a shelf

If you have the space, you can create a shelf, or clear the top of a cabinet and you can place your dog's special items grouped together. I've seen some nice ones of these. You can have your friend's ashes displayed next to a photo and their collar. Some people burn candles for remembrance too. It becomes a focal point for your beloved friend.

Lynda has created a little memory shrine in her dining room for Buttons. She has a memory box, with paw prints, and she is surrounded by her special things and photos.

Plant a tree or a flower

My Mum and Dad had my childhood friend, a beautiful golden retriever named Teddie, cremated when he fell asleep in 1995, then they placed his urn at the bottom of the garden and planted a beautiful yellow rose in his honour. When they moved at the start of 2016 they took the rose bush with them. At the very least you're able to take cuttings of a plant or a bush if you move house.

Perhaps you can turn a little part of your garden into a memory corner for your dog or lost pets and decorate it with things they would have enjoyed, or little plaques in their honour. Liz has placed Sara's ashes in the garden and brought a lovely plant to mark the area. A water feature is another lovely idea you can try.

Plaques

You should be able to locate may places that will engrave a plaque for you at a reasonable price – try a jewellery shop or the little shops that duplicate keys. Decide what you would like on a plaque and write it down and take this with you for reference. Check the spelling! You can either have the plaque fixed to a memento or keepsake, or you can find photo frames with areas to be engraved.

Write poetry or a tribute

I wrote a poem for Herbie. I have no idea where it is now, probably buried in the recesses of the memory of my lap top. As you know, I also wrote a few blogs, journal entries and letters. These things weren't really for anyone else, they were for me and him. They helped me to touch him with my mind, and work through his absence. You can do the same thing. You may not feel that you are eloquent or that you can write, but believe me, everything you need will come from the heart. You can publish a tribute on Facebook for your friends to see, as Helen did, and that can be cathartic and comforting.

Keep a journal if you like. Write down how you're feeling, and what your memories are. Things will come back to you at different stages and they'll make you smile and make you cry. You don't have to show anyone else, you don't have to publish it. But if you do want to, you can. The choice is yours. In terms of poetry, you could publish your poem to one of the Facebook pages that I've included in the useful support links at the end of this book, where I am sure your poetry would be warmly received, especially if you add a photo of your friend. If you wish to write a little memoir, it is possible to publish on Kindle with very little fuss, as long as you don't expect great plaudits or financial reward. It's nice to have something to show friends.

Alternatively, you can do a really good job, hire an editor and a proof reader, buy an ISBN number and have a cover designed and really go out on a limb with it. It's entirely up to you. This little book is in many ways my tribute to Herbie, isn't it?

Jewellery

There are a number of companies that specialise in turning ashes into jewellery that you may be interested in. Or you can find companies that place ashes into little jewellery keepsakes. Many types of jewellery can be customized with your dog's information or photograph. Jewellery types range from pendants and charms to actual paw print and nose print engravings and come in stainless steel, pewter, gold and silver.

Window Decals

My dog groomer has a window decal in the back of her car, honouring the beloved boy she lost in 2015. You can apply window decals to windows or other smooth surfaces and the best thing is you get to completely personalise them with your dog's name and dates, or simply a message.

Taxidermy

For some people the thought of burying or cremating their dog is just too traumatic and they opt for taxidermy instead. I have checked and that option is available in the UK and the US but bear in mind that it is very expensive and many taxidermists no longer offer the service? Why? Well because the way your pet looked in life is very difficult to capture once s/he is stuffed. Your expectations may be too high or unrealistic. I think you would need to think hard about this option, because if you want to remember your best friend in a particular way, you don't want the results of poor taxidermy forever clouding your memories.

Tattoo

A tattoo is a permanent reminder of your dog – you could have his or her face engraved somewhere you can see it, or simply paw prints or a saying, or your dog's name and their dates, or a feather (as many people believe a white feather is a symbol of the beyond).

Memory shrine

Heather buried Diggs in a substantial homemade coffin, six feet down and covered by stainless steel and concrete. She says, "all our lost dogs have a memorial plate on the garden wall. There's a water feature dedicated to them too. We will never move."

Do something in honour of your dog's memory

You've probably already done something like this, but occasionally I send PayPal donations to various rescues and just add, 'Sent in memory of Herbie' to the recipient. You could donate to any cause close to your heart, send dog food or blankets and toys to a local kennel for example, or even run for an animal charity. You know your best friend would approve.

Longer term strategy

Anniversaries, birthdays etc., are all going to knock you for six. One way to deal with these is to try to forget them. I know, I know!

A more helpful suggestion is to reprogram yourself to see them as celebrations. This is only a half-formed thought in my mind at the moment, as I come up to Herbie's first anniversary. However, I am intending to walk in his honour, take some flowers to our special place and tie a blue ribbon to our tree. I'm publishing this little book and maybe I'll cook a nice dinner and share some wonderful memories of him with my husband and other dogs. I'm going to tell myself over and over that I was fortunate to have shared nearly ten years with the most amazing creature. And I'm going to buy some cheese and ham snacks and stuff my face because for some reason he really loved those in the last few weeks before he passed.

Yes. From now on, July 29th will be Herbie day and I will celebrate his life and our love!

There's no rush

Remember, you can take your time to decide exactly how you want to create a memorial for your pet, if indeed you do. It can take time to decide what to do and when to do it. Barney is still at home with Libby, "it's way too early for me to do anything yet, but I will be planting a tree in the garden and he will rest there with my cat Paddy, whom I lost in 2016. They were best buddies."

17. A NEW BEST FRIEND?

Should you find yourself a new best friend? The answer to this of course, is that it is an entirely individual decision.

You will know when the time is right to find a new best friend. In my case I couldn't countenance a world without a friend to love who would love me back (I hoped) and so I started looking very quickly. I took my lurcher puppy, Finley, four weeks after I lost Herbie. Boy, did I cry on the drive home though. I was full of love for my new friend and love for my old friend, and still grieving.

I can let you know why it worked for me though, it's a perfect distraction from your own feelings, and of course you have so much to do with a puppy anyway. I was moving house, looking after our business, and looking after a puppy and I was run ragged. I was in deep pain, often completely detached and numb, but also strangely happy at times. My husband was less thrilled. He was painting the new house, and Finley and the paint pots didn't mix. I'd often come home from work and find Fin with fresh white patches on his fur.

Choosing a new best friend was right for me.

It was right for Lynda too. After the loss of Buttons, she found Willow, and like me, has found that a dog with a very different personality does help.

Liz also opted for a new puppy, the same breed as Sara. "A baby Sara." She notes the drawbacks though. "Even that caused me problems when things were not going right and made me yearn back to Sara, but Sage our puppy, has filled an awful emptiness. She keeps me busy and has a lot of love to give, and we have our walks again, so routine is back." It was the best thing she could do, Liz says. "I would like to say that time always heals and it does but for the first time in my life, having had family bereavements where that applies, I found losing my dog wasn't the same. Each person is different. Some may need to get another dog. Some may want to wait. Some may start to enjoy the freedom of not being tied. My advice would be that if you still miss your dog so much and the pain isn't going away then you have nowhere else to turn except to get another."

Heather made a decision she says, that shocked her. "After a month of mourning, my heart ached to cuddle another boy. By accident or coincidence, I was on a dog based forum when someone came on looking for a new home for a 12-week-old puppy. I couldn't believe it. I messaged the person immediately and said we would have him. My husband was shocked I had done this but he said, "I think you need a new young dog in your life," and we went and brought the puppy home. He took so much time, energy, and care. It gave me little time to think about anything else. And he made us laugh. We could laugh and we loved this new little life that was full of energy and we shared his awe as he explored his new world."

How do you know if looking for a new puppy is the right thing for *YOU?*

Consider what it means having a new puppy in your life. It's messy. It's time consuming. They are destructive. They cost a lot of money. They have to be trained. They take time, effort and patience. Do you have all of those things to offer?

Perhaps you could have a rescue? If you're choosing a rescue, be extremely sure. A rescue has had a hard life already; you don't want to let her down again. Some rescue dogs also come with their own fair share of issues and challenges, so make sure you understand exactly what they are. It's not a no-go area though, and can be really good for you and your new friend. I highly recommend rescuing (after all Toby and Satin were rescues). You can always access help through a dog behavioural expert if you need to, and it's hugely rewarding to rehome a dog.

If you already have a dog or dogs, are you certain that they will welcome a new arrival? Especially so soon after the loss of a member of the pack. I had this challenge. Satin was a little unnerved by the newbie (after all she's thirteen or fourteen) and Betsy my Bedlington terrier was very snappy. So we had some fisticuffs and needed help from the Vet. We used Adaptil and that seemed to keep things calm. We have a little lip curling now from time to time, mainly over food, but John and I are quick learners.

If you are rescuing, make sure any existing dogs you have, meet the new one first. See how they get on before you make a firm decision. Some dogs get on, and some don't.

Why you might not want a new best friend

If it's been a while since you had a puppy, your circumstances might have changed. You may have moved house, retired, changed job, had children etc. Make the decision based on practical considerations rather than emotional ones. This is a real case of 'do as I say and not as I do' though. My heart ruled my head when Finley came home with us, but I don't regret it.

When we lose people we don't replace them because we can't. You can't bring your best friend back. I know this, because I've tried, but Herbie was not Toby, and Finley is not Herbie.

It may be challenging for any existing dogs you have. They may become aggressive or dejected.

At the end of the day, the decision is yours and yours alone, but here's my thoughts from a blog I wrote at the end of August 2016, five weeks after I lost Herbie.

The Writer's Apprentice

*It was never a matter of **if**, and always a case of **when**, and so this weekend, my husband and I did a 530-mile round trip in 24 hours to collect a little bundle of fluff. We ummed and ahhed quite a lot. Was it too soon? Yes. Was he too far away? Definitely. Was I trying to find Herbie? Maybe. Was he the right dog? Who knows! But there he was, sticking his tongue out at me via the wonders of the Tinterweb, and I just knew he was the one. What if I let him pass and never found the right pup? I'm terrible for worrying about such things, and so insurmountable barriers had to be surmounted, and that's what* *we did.*

It's a bizarre thing to be grieving for your BFFF (best furry friend forever) and yet to be cradling this tiny ball of wonder. He is a salve to my crushed heart, Aloe Vera for my burning soul. But that's not to say the pain of Herbie's loss has faded, because it really, really hasn't. This morning I had a puppy on the bed for the first time in years, and although I was knackered and it was far too early, he was funny and he made me laugh … and then my eyes strayed to the bedroom door where Herbie would have been standing, issuing me a cool stare that said, "Are you getting up then, or what? I want my walk." It's been the same every morning since that final day (17 days now actually, not that I'm counting). My eyes flick there and he's not there, and that's when I weep for the first time every day, without fail.

But I'm going about my business better than I was, trying to catch up on the backlog of work.

Then mid-afternoon, a song came on the radio that I like and I picked the puppy up and cradled him and we had a little dance and I sang gently in his ear, my lips close to his soft cheek, and it was joyous to be in the moment with him … and I cried like a baby for the boy I used to do that with. Even fully grown (and he was quite a big lad, my Herbie) he LOVED to do that. We would pretend he was a puppy all over again.

And just now, I sat in the sunshine with a cup of tea after exploring the garden with the puppy and then I cried, because the sky was so beautifully blue and the sun so warm, and my sweet Herbie is dust in a casket in the living room, his name beautifully engraved on a brass plaque. And I miss him. I bloody miss him.

121

So, a puppy? What the hell was I thinking of?

Puppies are chaotic, but their development is incredibly swift. So far, in 24 hours, this new lad has learned how to do the steps to outside. He knows where the water bowl is. He can do wee wees and poo poos in the garden, but has the occasional accident in the hall. He comes when I call, 'puppy'. We haven't finalised his name quite yet. He's a marvel.

He has explored all the rooms, but is still a little shy about certain things and follows me around like a tiny fluffy shadow. Our old dog (Satin) is a sweetheart; she's Grandma – gives him a wash when she can be bothered. Our Bedlington Terrier (Betsy) is having a right mard because: a) we left her in kennels overnight while we raced up country and how very, very dare we! And b) "I'm the puppy!"

Now she knows how Herbie felt when we brought her home. Bless her.

I have remembered how to do 'the puppy shuffle'. This involves walking around as though wearing a large nappy, so that when he dives between your feet there's enough space so that you don't crush him to death, or kill yourself when you trip over him. His teeth and nails are like razors. My legs are covered in scratches because he likes to jump up at me. I like all of this.

I'm constantly confused about what and how much he needs to eat. I have a feeling he could just eat all day, but surely that wouldn't be good? I need to take advice on this. Betsy was a big eater, Herbie wasn't. Puppy is going to make 22-25 inches so he'll be pretty tall.

I laughed out loud (and alone) when puppy dashed out of the kitchen with the tea-towel clamped in his jaws. I'd just dropped it and off he flew, superfast. Jesus. This boy is going to be Usain Bolt. I was less enamoured when he decided he preferred my specs (Gok Wans – bought when I actually had a salary and could afford decent specs!) to his chewie toy however, and rapidly retrieved them, only to find he had them again the next time I looked his way. And he has an obsession with paper ... he finds it, he tears it up ...

My specs. Paper.

Where is he now? Sound asleep (at last!) on my left hand side as I type at my desk. Let me repeat that. On my left hand side. Do you have any idea how that makes me feel? You will if you read my last blog.

He's amazing and beautiful, I love him already, which is not to dishonour Herbie's memory in any way. I hope not anyhow. I love Herbie as much as I ever did.

Let me introduce you to The Writer's Apprentice. I think I'm going to cry again.

You'll be pleased to know that eventually we settled on the name Finley for the puppy, and he is quite a character. Incredibly bright and extremely funny. He is attending dog school and he loves Flyball. He's a real tonic and I love him very much.

18. FINAL ADVICE FROM PEOPLE WHO HAVE BEEN WHERE YOU ARE NOW

Lynda, who lost Buttons in 2008, says that if she had to offer advice to other bereaved dog owners, it would be this. "Take time to grieve how you want to, don't let others dictate how you should feel, or how long you should feel like grieving. If you want to do a particular thing for your deceased pet, do it. Everyone is different.

"If you want another dog quickly go for it, if you need time, take the time. It is really hard losing a dog, they truly are your best friend, and a family member. There are many stages of grief and not everyone goes through all the stages, but do what you need to do, and above all look after yourself.

"If people don't understand, or make inappropriate comments, don't take it to heart, it took me a long time to realise that they have not had the privilege of sharing a part of their life with one of the most wonderful creatures you could ever love."

Sarah who lost Dirk in 2017, advises that people should, "keep telling themselves that they did everything they could have done, that their dog had a great life, and there was nothing more that could have been done. To look at videos of them running about when young healthily and happily, it really heartens the soul to remember them like that."

125

Sarah adds, "Dirk was very sick with heart disease and auto-immune – a friend of mine said that you get given the dog you have learned to be able to cope with, and I found that a very moving thought."

Libby has had many pets over the years, and knows loss comes with the territory but it still hurts. "Having lost other pets (dogs/horses/cats) I know the pain gets easier to deal with. I feel you just have to hold on to the time you had with them and remember all the good bits, their quirky ways, the fun and unconditional love they give. But most importantly I feel very strongly that they choose you as much as you choose them."

Helen who is still getting to grips with the loss of Poppy so recently, advises, "To try not to have feeling of guilt. It is easy to say, and we all do it, but I think that is the one thing that destroys us. Make time and allow yourself to grieve for however long it takes. Do not be put off by people saying you should be over it by now. Think often of your dog, even stroke that dog and talk to it, anything that makes you feel closer to your dog."

Heather suggests it is important to try not to dwell on the last days of your dog's life. "Think only of the happy days. And whilst it sounds selfish and cold, put your sad memories to one side. They will not help your beloved dog and they will not help you. And don't feel disloyal in taking in another dog. Think of it as a tribute to your lost boy."

Liz thanked me for the opportunity to write her thoughts down. "When my dog wasn't there it rocked my foundations and I found it difficult to cope with the slightest problem. I did, but it was a struggle and no one else knew but I prayed that nothing awful would happen because I knew I was just keeping my head above water and wouldn't be able to cope. Sage, our puppy, is helping me get back to the being the person I was where I can help others and be strong for them. All I need is that little person being strong for me at home at the end of the day.

"May I take this opportunity to say that whether you use this or not, you have helped me an awful lot by putting my grief down in writing and letting someone know how I have felt over losing my dog and it has helped so much. I am sure many other people will have benefited in the same way so I thank you very much for listening."

Thanks Liz. That goes for me too.

❋ ❋ ❋

Thanks to everyone who reads this book, everyone who will listen to what we bereaved owners have had to say. Writing and compiling **Losing my Best Friend** has been an honour.

19. ENDINGS AND BEGINNINGS

I don't really know how to end this book. I've never promised you that the pain goes away. I've said it eases. You regain your ability to function, but the pain of loss just remains a glowing ache. Sometimes it is hot and it lodges in your throat, other times it is cold and sits in your stomach, weighing you down. I trust that it lessens over time, but as of publication day for *Losing my Best Friend*, I am exactly twelve months in, and I can honestly say that I miss him now as much as I ever have.

My depression and anxiety are better, I can laugh and have fun, but every day, at least once, without fail, sometimes more often, I will stop what I'm doing and well up. My hands will be still but in my mind they are reaching for him, wanting to feel the silkiness of his gorgeous head.

You and I have travelled on a journey through the pages in this book, and between us we've probably cried buckets over the words contained herein. You've met Herbie and shared my pain, but I haven't met your best friend. I have written a blog post on my website especially for readers of this book to share memories of their best friends. I'd love you to come along and say, as I did at the start of this book, "Let me tell you about ...." And then post some memories and thoughts down, or come to Herbie's page on Facebook – search for **Herbie Longfellow Alderdice** - and post your memories of your dog there.

Equally if you have advice to share with others who have lost their best friends, tell me that too. The detail in this book will need updating and I'll be looking for ideas about what helped you in the aftermath of losing your best friend.

Thank you for listening to my 'tails' about Herbie, and thank you for reading. I'll close by saying that wherever you are, whoever you are, no matter how old you are, whether you're a man or woman or someone in between, and no matter what your religious beliefs – you are amazing. You loved a creature who loved you back. You loved them so much that your heart is almost irreparably broken. That doesn't make you 'sad', or a 'loser', or 'oversensitive', or 'crazy' or anything else anyone may have called you. You have kept your best friend's memory aflame and that makes you super special.

Your dog was never just a dog, he or she was your best friend.

I'm sending out hugs and best wishes to you all.

Jeannie xxx

20. ONLINE RESOURCES FOR PET BEREAVEMENT

There are so many resources available on the Internet. I don't suggest Googling loads and reading them all and making yourself sad, although you can if you like, but here are a few which may help you.

The Blue Cross

https://www.bluecross.org.uk/pet-bereavement-support

The Blue Cross provide free and confidential emotional support to anyone who is affected by the loss of a pet, and have a range of literature available that you can download. They can also offer support if your dog or another pet is terminally ill and you are unsure when to say goodbye. The Blue Cross is a charity, and lines are manned by volunteers. Calls are free in the UK on 0800 096 6606.

You may also email them: pbssmail@bluecross.org.uk You can expect a response within 48 hours.

There is a facility to create an online pet memorial, if you feel this would help.

Living with Pet Bereavement

http://www.livingwithpetbereavement.com/

Living with Pet Bereavement offers pet carers a lifeline, advice, information and support during the time it takes them to come to terms with their loss.

You can access:

- Pre, during and post euthanasia support and advice.

- Online memorial pages dedicated to your pets.

- Memorial products.

Pet Loss Help

http://www.petlosshelp.org/home.html

Pet Loss Help have a range of online resources, along with a Hall of Fame and a Blog.

Prayers for Pets

http://prayersforpets1.org/

A non-profit organization dedicated to ministering to the needs of hurting pets and their families, who also lend spiritual support, guidance, counsel and information. You can request prayers.

The Ralph Site

http://www.theralphsite.com/

The Ralph site is a not-for-profit website that provides support to pet carers around the loss of a beloved companion. Resources that you might find helpful include information on euthanasia and aftercare options, managing your grief, and ideas for memorials. You can create an online memorial on the website.

There are private forums, as well as an active and helpful private Facebook page, and a list of counsellors.

The Facebook link is:
https://www.facebook.com/groups/theralphsite/

Bogie and Ozzy's Rainbow Bridge

For a fun and supportive Rainbow Bridge website, check out this Facebook group:
https://www.facebook.com/groups/163834693810579/

Support Line

http://www.supportline.org.uk/problems/bereavement_p ets.php

Support Line offer a confidential telephone helpline offering emotional support to any individual on any issue, including pet bereavement. The Helpline is primarily a preventative service and aims to support people before they reach the point of crisis. SupportLine is a member of the Helplines Association.

Support Line also provides support by email and post.

Marie Pure

I mentioned that I used Bach flowers to help me with my overwhelming emotions. If you are interested in using Bach flowers to ease your grief, I recommend Marie Pure.

They do have a specific mix (Bach flowers mix no.68 for bereavement) but Tom created a personal mix for me, to help me deal with my anxiety, as it was out of control. You may want something that calms you down, or helps you sleep.

A Bach flowers mix will help you

- Deal with the shock of the death of your dog

- Soothe your grief

- Reduce anger and aggression (I found the mix really helped me with this)

- Help you to accept the death of your best friend

- Overcome your fears

Bach flowers are a naturalistic remedy, working in harmony with your body. They cause no side effects at all. I had a three-month course and felt better within six weeks, but it varies according to the individual.

If you are interested, check out the website https://www.bachfloweradvice.co.uk/

Then contact Tom and ask for a personal mix. He'll want to know what emotions you are feeling. Be open and honest – he's sympathetic. Please tell him hi from me!

The Cinnamon Trust

Further details about The Cinnamon Trust can be found online at http://www.cinnamon.org.uk/home.php

Or you can call 01736 757 900
General Enquiries Monday – Friday, 9am - 5pm
Emergency Calls available 24hrs

Herbie Longfellow Alderdice

If you would like to share your thoughts about ***Losing my Best Friend***, or memories of your pet, please drop me a line on Herbie's Facebook page. After all, if I don't keep it active, it will be closed down! You can find us here: https://www.facebook.com/Herbiethecaninepoet/

ACKNOWLEDGEMENTS

This book has been an incredible challenge, and several times I wanted to stop writing it. I have spent many an afternoon gazing into space, tears rolling down my cheeks, a pile of tissues to my side, and my fingers inches away from the keyboard, unable to 'perform'.

My love for Herbie and desire to share my feelings could only take me so far, but then other dog owners shared their stories with me - and suddenly I wasn't so alone, and I wanted to do them justice too.

I would like to thank the following for being brave enough to share their stories with such love and honesty: Lynda Cottrell and Buttons; Helen Houseman and Poppy; Sarah and Dirk; Liz and Sara; Libby Hammond and Barney; and Heather and Diggs.

I also owe a debt of gratitude to **The Bedlington/Whippet Pet Group** on Facebook for all their support and love for Herbie and I, in the days of his final illness and his passing.

Also the **Ralph Site Facebook Group** who have been tremendous and understanding in the aftermath of losing my precious boy. You can go in there every day, forever, and no-one will think you're crazy for still missing your beloved best friend, even several years on.

I need to thank Jennifer Syme, who told me about the waves analogy, and Janet Baird and the other Urban

Writers in the Writers' Playground, for their ongoing support. They've kept me going with all of my writing projects, in spite of my poor mood and lack of motivation at times.

Also a big shout out to my Mum and Dad, Rich, and John for their constant and unconditional love for me and for Herbie.

Thanks to Honiton Small Animal Clinic for their care of Herbie, and for holding my hand while championing Herbie's cause.

And thanks – most especially - to you, for reading this book and taking our stories to your heart.

Here's to our best friends - wherever they may be! ♥

ABOUT THE AUTHOR

Jeannie Wycherley is a writer, copywriter and gift shop proprietor who resides somewhere between the forest and the coast in East Devon, UK.

Her creative work is inspired by the landscape, not least because her desk affords her sweeping views over a valley and the glorious hills beyond. Why this translates into horror is anybody's guess.

She lives quietly with her husband and three dogs, enjoys making soup, reading and watching films. She thinks there is no greater honour than being a dog mama.

Find out more at on the website
https://www.jeanniewycherley.co.uk/

You can tweet Jeannie @thecushionlady

Or visit her on Facebook for her fiction
https://www.facebook.com/jeanniewycherley/

Visit Herbie's page to talk about Losing my Best Friend at
https://www.facebook.com/Herbiethecaninepoet/

Thanks!

Jeannie Wycherley

OTHER BOOKS BY JEANNIE WYCHERLEY

If you would like to read some of Jeannie's fiction, you'll find the following available:

Crone (2017)

Deadly Encounters (2017)

A Concerto for the Dead and Dying (2018)

Beyond the Veil (2018)

Please visit Jeannie's website for more updates

MAY I ASK A FAVOUR?

If you enjoyed this book, found it useful or otherwise, then I'd really appreciate it if you would post a short review on Amazon. I do read all the reviews personally so that I can write more of what people like.

If you'd like to leave a review, then please head to Amazon and find this book, and follow the instructions.

Thanks for your support!

Made in the USA
Las Vegas, NV
18 September 2021

30565518R00085